# ENJOYMENT AND
# THE ACTIVITY OF MIND

# VIBS

Volume 100

Robert Ginsberg
**Executive Editor**

a volume in
**Philosophy of Education**
**PHED**
George David Miller, Editor

# ENJOYMENT AND THE ACTIVITY OF MIND

## Dialogues on Whitehead and Education

Foster N. Walker

Amsterdam - Atlanta, GA 2000

The paper on which this book is printed meets the requirements of "ISO 9706:1994, Information and documentation - Paper for documents - Requirements for permanence".

ISBN: 90-420-1312-5
©Editions Rodopi B.V., Amsterdam - Atlanta, GA 2000
Printed in The Netherlands

To my daughter, friend, and teacher, Nicholette

# CONTENTS

# EDITORIAL FOREWORD

Foster N. Walker rises to the same challenge that Alfred North Whitehead faced in his writings on education: to explain and examine philosophical ideas without recourse to technical terms or elaborate forms of argument. By confining himself to everyday language, Walker renders fundamental educational questions and reflections accessible to all who are involved and interested in educational practice. His careful reassessment of the conceptual grounds which govern what transpires in schools and universities will prove of immediate value to those who endeavor to educate. To achieve the clarity and precision of thought requisite of such philosophic inquiry, yet to carry this out in the form of ordinary English discourse, is a daunting task. Walker succeeds admirably.

*Enjoyment and the Activity of Mind* offers an elaboration and application of the central ideas of Whitehead's *The Aims of Education and Other Essays*. Walker provides, however, more than an exegesis. The journal entries and dialogues exemplify many of Whitehead's conceptual constructs. The three sections of Walker's book, for example, illustrate Whitehead's three stages of mental growth. "David Ryan's Journal" corresponds to the romance stage, characterized by the glimmering excitement of Ryan's growing realization that there is something he wants to understand. "The Dialogues" are examples of the stage of precision: the gathering and marshaling of facts, and the critical scrutiny of organizing concepts. "The Journal Dialogues" portray the stage of generalization, as acquired understanding is applied to practice and extended to further realms of inquiry. It is a remarkable experience to read Walker's book and to recognize its ideas realized in the structure of the work itself.

Constructing his book as a series of journal entries and dialogues allows Walker to portray the reflective thought processes of a number of individuals. Reading the work is like peering into other minds, encountering there many of the same moments of excitement, frustration, error, and insight characteristic of our own inner dialogues. More than individual thought is conveyed however. Walker ably elaborates the rich mixture and interaction of ideas which derive from dialogue, and which lead to a more thorough understanding shared among participants. The effectiveness of dialogue as a means of educating is made apparent; so too is its potential to increase the quality of human life.

*Enjoyment and the Activity of Mind* is a finely crafted work. Its language and form readily engage us in the philosophic consideration of those ideas which ground all educational endeavor. As we read, we are invited to participate in the long, ongoing dialogic inquiry into education, an inquiry as exciting and necessary today as it was when Socrates first raised his questions.

Moya Kavanagh

# PREFACE

No doubt there is a story and a motivation of personal interest behind any creative work, a story that can illuminate the work itself. Certainly it is true of this book. Two years after leaving school, I was studying for a degree in chemistry while working in an industrial chemical laboratory. Academically, I was succeeding, which gave me the satisfaction of renewed confidence after sliding into unaccustomed failure toward the end of school. But it was, as always, largely memory work and the mechanical application of formulae, so that success was the fruit of grinding discipline in the midst of boredom. My interest in chemistry itself, kindled in a boy's chemistry set, had long ago expired in cramming for examinations at school. I had unwittingly succumbed to the cynical persuasion that mind should be used minimally for the pragmatic and cunning pursuit of career success. With the exception of the peculiar adventures of a few intellectual prodigies, I accepted that the enjoyment of life cannot arise from activity of mind.

By great good fortune, this assumption, as common as it is deadly, was unexpectedly and permanently obliterated. I never knew what caused it, but quite suddenly an intense energy of inquiry began to flow, and on it I floated gladly in the growing debris of former certainties. I started filling notebooks with original ideas, exhilarated by this spontaneous stream of insights, questions, and unfamiliar connections. Short stories also emerged, and then poetry. I became a regular patron of the library for the first time, taking out books on theology, psychology, philosophy of religion, and anything relevant to the questions arising in me. I had no explanation for them, and felt no need for one. I was enjoying my immersion in the process, unreflective about the strangeness of inquiry when impelled by nothing but my own sense of its importance. No one was working to motivate me, to punish me if I didn't do it, or to reward me if I did do it. With this activity of mind, the enjoyment of it was enough. Its energy, spontaneous and as naturally vitalizing as blood flowing in the arteries, was yet so unfamiliar that it was as if an old me had quietly slid away into the past.

Reflecting on this, I realized that although for me the awakening of the mind took a philosophical turn, for others it might be in the fine arts, or science, or business. The initial or predominant focus is not the point. What matters is the new quality of life when the mind is fulfilling its proper nature as an activity of inquiry, that is, when we are no longer accepting what we have been told about life in general and our individual lives. Instead, we feel impelled to find out for ourselves. Of necessity, the life of infants is suffused with this quality, but we later become so removed from it that we cannot respect it as an essential aspect of human life, without which we are living a kind of inner death.

This experiential rediscovery of the power and beauty of mind, as inquiry empowered and directed by the inner necessity of personal interest, became for me the source of a new perspective on schooling and education. I realized that my schooling had systematically retarded the development of my powers of understanding and jaded my attitude toward learning. It had confused mind with a combination of memory and some routine applications of stored information. It had confused training with educating and constricted intelligence to a trickle of pragmatic necessities and cunning diversions.

I came to see that the problem was not just my particular schooling but, with notable exceptions, schooling everywhere, and I no longer accepted the common assumption that schools just have to be this way. They will remain so, however, as long as a lack of deep inquiry persists in those influencing the direction of education. The wrong conception of the mind to be educated has persisted throughout the history of public education and continues to govern its aims and methods to this day.

I moved rapidly from chemical industry into school teaching, wanting to give others what I had been denied. To some extent I was successful, but overall my understanding was a muddle of old and new, and my pedagogical imagination was restricted by the patterns of my own schooling. I needed help to align my whole understanding around my discovery but did not see this consciously enough to plan appropriate action. Instead, the solution came unexpectedly when I returned to university after several years of teaching, with no purpose other than the satisfaction of a growing desire to immerse myself in literature and philosophy.

Two encounters there precipitated a quantum leap in my grasp of the purpose and practice of educating. One was the introduction to dialogue, in the form of the Socratic dialogues, and the other was the introduction to the writings of Alfred North Whitehead. Intrigued by Socrates' unique approach to teaching, I realized that dialogic inquiry has great power to fire the vitality of mind that I had experienced and which constituted my central concern as an educator. To my professors' dismay, I began writing my papers as imaginary dialogues, a practice that greatly clarified my ideas about using dialogue to evoke the learning whose most difficult phases are still vital and imperative.

Along with Socrates, the study of Whitehead's ideas was a philosophic and educational turning point for me. Historic and twentieth century writers on education had greatly helped me, but reading Whitehead's *The Aims of Education and Other Essays* was like finally and unexpectedly arriving at a long-sought destination. He put his finger immediately on the problem of mind in education, expressing it with a force, simplicity, and clarity for which I had struggled in vain. His central concern was mine: the inert and the alive mind and their diametrically opposed consequences for students, teachers, and the whole society. With the ease of a great philosopher and experienced educator, and the passion of a concerned humanitarian, he moved confidently and un-compromisingly back and forth from ideas to practice. His fluent prose took me quickly and surely to my areas of confusion and to the depth of great ideas where I was still paddling discontentedly in shallow waters. With the resources of *The Aims* I was gradually seeing how to gain the clarity of systematizing my ideas into an educational philosophy of my own and how to apply them in a reconception of practice from the ground upwards.

But why, I wondered, did Whitehead not feature in the studies of teacher-training colleges? Why had I heard nothing of him in the world of school teaching? Why did university teachers seem unaware of his illuminating essays on the real purpose of university education? I had a similar question about Socrates and dialogue. Why was Socrates' great discovery and demonstration of dialogue unknown among teachers, and kept at a safe theoretical distance in the resolutely didactic pedagogy of philosophy departments? Whatever the reasons, as soon as I entered the world of philosophy teaching and teacher education I began experimenting with dialogic approaches and with the addition of *The Aims* to course literature.

The opportunity for dialogue has always been immediately welcomed by students, but their continuing discomfort with *The Aims* forced me to stand back and reassess it as it appears to others. The difficulty of grasping the full perspective from which his statements emerge rapidly extinguished the initial interest in Whitehead's forthright language. Although Whitehead was speaking in *The Aims* as a teacher to teachers, he was also thinking as a philosopher, with a complex mind and a desire to make a deep critical assessment within the daunting parameters of non-technical language and the brevity of single lectures. The resulting density of ideas in every paragraph made it necessary for me to take students through a long, step-by-step analysis, and I had to sup-plement Whitehead's brief practical elaboration of his ideas with streams of examples capturing the details of the immediate experience of institutional teaching and learning.

My attempts to provide helpful reading for these points of difficulty were largely unsuccessful. Most of the writing about Whitehead's educational es-says is far too abstract, technical, and distant from the practical concerns of teachers. It does not exhibit Whitehead's meaning in the details of the immedi-ate life of the teacher, and it rarely addresses educational problems as teachers and students would voice them. Contemplating the problem, I decided to at-tempt a book capturing, for thoughtful teachers and educators of teachers, something of the way in which I had managed, eventually, to bring Whitehead permanently alive for many practicing educators. I do not mean a lively memory sitting on an academic shelf gathering dust along with other mementos of the intellectual sampling of educational theories. I refer to an encounter with Whitehead sufficiently arresting to throw a whole educational life into question, and sufficiently complete to show in the manner of the encounter a way to move the energy constructively into the creation of a personal philosophy that safeguards the most precious quality of mind. The challenge here is not to become a true believer in Whitehead or my interpretation of him. It is the challenge to engage deeply with a vision of educating for which Whitehead is the most clear and uncompromising exponent.

The purpose of the writing was clear enough to me. The dissatisfaction of the initial attempt brought me back to my other interest, namely, dialogue. I had experimented with different types of literature on the philosophic side of the student-teachers' program. The same ideas that proved stubbornly obscure in the specialist prose of textbooks and articles tended to yield their implications with ease in the dramatic concreteness and ordinary language of dialogic writing. In philosophy as a whole, such writing was available. But for Whitehead's educational ideas, I had found nothing similar. This realization provoked my desire to follow my earlier attempts at written dialogue and let the book consist of imaginary, enjoyable, and serious written dialogues. This approach had the added appeal of enabling me to illustrate in the writing itself the educational value of dialogue, especially for evoking the very activity of mind that is at issue. And the characters in the dialogues, though fictional inventions, easily took shape from my decades of direct involvement with teachers, education students, administrators, and parents.

Since the use of the word "dialogue" for almost any conversational interaction is so familiar, it might understandably be difficult to see why I would accord it emphasis beyond its potential for giving an ease of reading comparable to the ease of listening to a conversation. But the familiarity with the word is rarely accompanied by an appreciation of its distinctive meaning and significance as a mode of communication and joint inquiry. When distinguished from ordinary conversation, discussion, debate, and every other form of speech, dialogue is arguably the most neglected area of culture. It is therefore understandable for it to be the most neglected possibility of educational engagement. However, its enormous potential for organized learning, and for creating mutual understanding in the face of apparently intractable divisiveness, makes its neglect a serious human and educational problem. I have tried to demonstrate something of these potentials in the dialogues, though I make no attempt here to argue claims about dialogue. Suffice it to say that a careful study of the structure and dynamics of the dialogues, and Henry Freedman's facilitation of them, could reveal much to the reader interested in dialogue itself. As represented here, the patience, civility, and discipline of joint inquiry, without loss of an essential spontaneity, are not a misleading idealization, but a simplification of a living process in which I have participated countless times. Educational and cultural dialogue has been neglected and, due to general lack of experience, is difficult. But it is entirely possible.

For a long time, I had pursued Whitehead's ideas and the art of dialogue separately, not consciously realizing their intimate connection. Although Whitehead points to the value of open-minded exchange and other features of dialogue, he does not discuss dialogic inquiry as an approach remarkably suited to the practical realization of his educational vision. I would now claim that this vision cannot be put into practice without giving an honored place to dialogic learning in the daily activities of school and university. My hope is that the dialogues here will be considered in that light, and furnish a strong suggestion for an advance in pedagogical imagination and teacher education.

For the philosophically tuned reader, *The Aims* will suggest intriguing lines of epistemological and metaphysical investigation, as we might expect from a philosopher of Whitehead's standing. The exploration of these would certainly reveal much more of the depth and solidity of his position. But any inquiry of this sort, which we would find in, say, *Modes of Thought* and *Process and Reality*, is not the point of this work. Exploring, for example, the analogy between Whitehead's three stages of learning and the becoming and perishing of the "actual entities" constituting the cosmos, or the connection of art, beauty, and enjoyment in learning with the central place of aesthetic harmony in "concrescence," are journeys for which interested readers will find many able guides in academic literature.

My emphasis on *The Aims* as the book devoted primarily to Whitehead's educational ideas should not be taken as implying that it is the only source. Other valuable educational essays are available in *Whitehead's American Essays in Social Philosophy*, and *Science and the Modern World*, both mentioned in the text. An essay on science education is in *Alfred North Whitehead: The Interpretation of Science; Selected Essays*, edited by A.H. Johnson. Some interesting remarks on education (and everything else in the world) are to be found in Lucien Price's *Dialogues of Alfred North Whitehead*. Whitehead comments on his own schooling and educational involvement in the "Autobiographical Notes" of *The Philosophy of Alfred North Whitehead*, edited by Paul Arthur Schilpp.

Finally, I would recommend that, since this book is not in the form of a textbook or scholarly monograph but a story, it should first be read as story. Readers should allow themselves to be drawn, as participant-observers, into the experience of the characters, feeling with them the potential of great ideas and authentic inquiry to change a life. When the story has been lived, as stories should be, the proper time has come to return to the beginning and join the inquiry as critical and scholarly thinkers active in the step-by-step scrutiny of detail.

# ACKNOWLEDGMENTS

Philip Wright of the Philosophy Department at the University of Winnipeg introduced me to a serious consideration of the depth and scope of the work of Alfred North Whitehead. Wright's inspired teaching irreversibly secured my interest in Whitehead, and his generous help as a mentor over years secured for me an understanding solid enough to continue my exploration indefinitely. I carry the memory of him with great affection.

In the University of Western Ontario's Philosophy Department, the Whiteheadian scholar, A.H. Johnson, challenged me with wit and warmth for two hours every week over five years to defend my interpretation of Whitehead. His friendship and immense scholarship were offered unconditionally for my benefit. As with Wright, the very idea of this book is inconceivable without Johnson.

My thanks to Moya Kavanagh, formerly a philosopher in the University of Alberta. Kavanagh's appreciation of what I have attempted in this book, her tireless editing, and the professional quality of her philosophical and literary criticisms have been indispensable.

My gratitude to Karin Ruggeberg, who has read and listened to so much of my writing, and continually encouraged me with the reasoned perspective of an astute and educated sensibility in the domains of philosophy, psychology, and literary aesthetics.

I wish to thank Colleen Eggertson for the timely reminder of my love of writing in the form of dialogue. The initial attempt at this book in standard academic prose was so dissatisfying that I doubt if it would have been continued if Colleen had not asked me discerning questions about style in relation to my project.

My thanks to Owen Schwartz for important comments on the writing of the preface.

I am grateful to the (now sadly dissolved) Department of Educational Foundations in the University of Alberta for the freedom I had over twenty years to experiment continuously with new courses and pedagogical approaches, particularly those involving Whiteheadian ideas, group dialogue, and dialogue-journals with partners. My thanks also to Joyce Bainbridge for the benefit of her collaboration and enterprise in the initial research on pairing students for work on dialogue-journals. To my graduate and undergraduate students down the years, for their willingness and warm companionship in the risky adventure of open dialogue, my sincere thanks.

My thanks to Patrick deMaré, Peter Garrett, David Bohm, David Gilbert, Rob Abbott, Joyce Richman, Michael Tacon, and Lynne Walker, for expediting critical refinements of my understanding and practice of group dialogue.

Thanks to Robert Ginsberg and George David Miller of the Value Inquiry Book Series for their friendly and generous editing and support throughout the preparation of the manuscript.

# PART 1

## Meditations of a Dissatisfied Teacher

# One

# DAVID RYAN'S JOURNAL

### 24 September

I don't know if writing my thoughts down will help, but Louise is sure it will. She says keeping a journal gradually turns complaints into something constructive. Maybe. I don't know. Anyway, she won't listen to my dissatisfactions anymore, and I can't think of anyone else, so I suppose I'd better give writing a try. Just write anything that comes to mind, she said, and let it flow on without any effort to make it into something. Well, what is on my mind? Oh, yes—Harry.

My disagreement with Harry, who teaches grade six, bothers me. It keeps returning to me as an obsessive sort of "being bothered." My thoughts keep going back to Harry whether I like it or not. I wonder what that is? What comes to mind now is that conversation with him as we got coffee in the staff room. I remarked that I think something is wrong with our curriculum subjects because my grade five students don't like them. Or rather, they can get interested in questions of social justice or math puzzles if they happen to turn up by surprise. But when it comes to announcing time for math, I feel a universal "turn-off" in the class. It's like the peculiarity of all those night-singing insects when I was in Hong Kong which suddenly lapsed into absolute silence all at the same instant—millions of them together.

"So what's new, Ryan?"—those were Harry's words. How it irritates me the way he always calls me by my last name. I don't know how well I can remember what he said, but it was close to this: "Subjects mean disciplined thinking, and kids prefer to ramble around on whatever strikes them in the moment. But that's not really thinking. It's kicking ideas around aimlessly like four-year-olds pretending to play soccer. That's what we have school for— to stop them rambling aimlessly for the rest of their lives and then wondering why their lives go nowhere." I replied, "You mean a 'subject' is itself a discipline of thinking? But do we need subjects for thought to be disciplined to get real results? What exactly is a 'subject' supposed to be—once you try to get past the names, like math and science? And the curriculum exercises in them—what are they supposed to achieve?"

"Ryan, are you having me on?" he asked in an incredulous tone. "I cherish my bit of recess for important things like cigarettes and coffee, and you ask me what a subject is? A subject is what we do in math, or science, or grammar. What could be more obvious? Kids don't like discipline, that's all.

And nowadays they aren't prepared to simply get moving on the say-so of
authority figures like you and me. So we have to frighten them into it with
failure, or find a way to make it interesting, but however we do it, just do it.
If your job is lifting heavy boxes, just lift them. Don't keep complaining
about your weight loss in perspiration. Or else go and push paper, which is
light, or be a hermit in a cave. There's the buzzer. Damn, and I haven't drunk
my coffee; it's cold, and it's your fault."

So there it is. He doesn't want to think about it. I can't stop myself
thinking about it. Where do I go from here?

Just wandered around a bit looking for inspiration and pulled out a book
on my shelves which has sat there unread since university days: A.H. Johnson's *Whitehead's American Essays in Social Philosophy*. I turned to
"Historical Changes." It seems to be an essay on the educational importance of
history. I'm stuck on one statement and can't get past it. "As we think, we
live," says Whitehead. I was trying to get an answer to what a "subject" is,
really, and why it's supposed to be so important in teaching that I have to be a
slave-driver, even a kind one, which I don't like. I suppose I could be in the
wrong job. Anyway, this one statement seemed glued in my mind, and I forgot all the rest. Does that mean I am an undisciplined thinker?

"As we think, we live." For some reason I take thinking to be important, and teaching thinking, I assume, is important in education, and not just
because people are always saying that. I find myself somewhat in awe of people who really seem to be able to think.

I want to know what Whitehead means in that statement. I would have
said, "As we live, we think," but he doesn't, and I'm sure he doesn't mess
around with word order. What's the difference? As I live from day to day,
sleeping, teaching, grocery shopping, I think. I think about the shopping and
often lose that to a thought about what I forgot to get at the drugstore, or a
thought about whether I should be jogging instead of watching TV. What are
these different thoughts drifting in and having to be dropped when I realize I've
lost my place on the shopping list? Perhaps it isn't so much thinking but
visualized anxieties clamoring for attention in my mind's eye? If that's right,
what is real thinking?

Here's a possibility. Perhaps Whitehead means something quite different,
like "as we think, so we live," meaning that in some way our lives take the
shape of our thoughts (but don't our thoughts also take the shape of our
lives?). Perhaps I can see what he's after. If I hadn't had an idea of going
shopping, I wouldn't have gone shopping. That's plain enough. But if we get
to something crucial, like World War II, we could say that if Hitler hadn't had
an idea about Aryan supremacy that war would never have occurred. That must
be what Whitehead is getting at. The way our lives shape themselves depends

on what ideas we cling to. You could say that the intentions which govern our actions are themselves shaped out of the ideas we believe are right. That fits with his next sentence: "The mind is the crucible in which we fashion our purposes."

But I'm sure Hitler's idea was false and evil. I can't see why being Aryan makes one superior, simply superior as a person, though it might make one superior perhaps in some specific area. And other races are superior in other areas. And it's evil because it brought untold suffering and death to millions, and all unnecessary. Could Whitehead be implying that whether life turns out to be good, bad, or indifferent depends on whether we have the right kind of ideas or not? That sounds correct, anyway. And then we could say that we teach in order to bring the right ideas to students. I see a snag here though. When we get past obviously good ideas like freedom from slavery, or obviously bad ideas like Hitler's, who are we to make the students' choices for them? What ideas are good? Or instead, what is the procedure for doing this? Is it a good idea to get married? To have marriage at all? Is it a good idea to have schools? (I hear that Ivan Illich in *Deschooling Society* is sure it isn't.)

Have I gone off on a tangent? Reading over this I see I was talking about "thoughts" and "thinking" but then moved on to "ideas," although they don't seem to be that different. A thought could be an idea, or rather, my having or thinking about an idea. Or would it be thinking with an idea? Is that it? Ideas are the content of what we think? Then would disciplined thinking be the process of being careful how we deal with ideas, and what ideas we choose to deal with? I seem to have lost "subjects." Another time. Goodnight journal.

## 26 September

I keep coming back in my mind to Harry's remark about motivating kids to do schoolwork without fuss by frightening them with the thought of failure. I know Harry has been in this work a long time, is respected by the students, and gets impressive results—of a sort, but this idea of frightening kids with failure just doesn't sound right to me.

I remember he also said "or interest them—or make it interesting," or something like that. Now with that I have no problem. I like to see kids working when they are really interested. And when they are interested they certainly do better work then than I would have expected. That's the bit of progressivism I definitely agree with. But when they work with a fear of failure isn't that also a kind of interest, though different? The first kind of interest sounds right to me, and the second kind sounds wrong—even if they get good exam results. What I keep remembering is how it exhausts me when I have had to work simply through fear, and how good I always feel when I work with my own personal interest right there in the learning itself. I wonder if the results are really that different.

I know, of course, that there are always rebellious kids who won't work even with the ax of failure above them. They just say, "I don't care about failing." And I know Harry knows this as well. Do we just let kids like that fail, and that's that? Or what?

### 27 September

I got drawn back to that Whitehead book again today, and saw in the "Preface" that he has another book entirely about education, *The Aims of Education and Other Essays*. I was getting excited thumbing through the used copy I picked up on the way home, and was stopped dead by two passages in Chapter Three. He says:

> There can be no mental development without interest. . . . You may endeavor to excite interest by means of birch rods, or you may coax it by the incitement of pleasurable activity. But without interest there will be no progress.

And then he adds, and get this: "Now the natural mode by which living organisms are excited towards suitable self-development is enjoyment." Enjoyment! That's personal interest, and according to him that is the way to learn, to grow, given by nature itself. If that is right, then making people work at learning by making them afraid of failure would be forcing them to go against the way nature has made them. I think I must have been trying to get at something like that, but I couldn't see it. Going against nature here must be a bit like trying to make people breathe with very little oxygen while working hard. They feel awful, like the Everest climbers, because it goes against the way they are made to function. The trouble that I see is: what child outside school would do school work by choice, from sheer personal interest? And yet a lot of this stuff really is important to learn, and you can't function in our world without it. Surely the whole human culture can't be against nature! That's too much to swallow.

I don't see how most of school work could be handled so as to feel interesting to the kids. I don't know; I'm lost at this point.

### 5 October

Sorry, Journal, I ignored you for a while. Just too busy, or too tired. Don't take it to heart!

As matter of fact, I have been waiting to get back to you for days. I was struck by another passage in that Whitehead book, in Chapter Seven, about universities. I wonder if I can get Harry to see some of this. Whitehead says: "You must be free to think rightly and wrongly, and free to appreciate the variousness of the universe undisturbed by its perils." That gives me an idea about my disagreement with Harry over fear as an incitement to learning. (I see I've written "incitement." Interesting. I would never have thought to use such a word before reading Whitehead. It's good to have just the right word handy.) Anyway, from the rest of what Whitehead says I gather that the general idea is that the advantage of a school (or university), if it's going properly, is that students can take a lot of risks in learning without there being the danger of awful consequences. Which is not like out-of-school life, because, for example, in school one could play around a bit with being a dictatorship, and the students will feel how bad it is to be arbitrarily pushed around, and so get the message. But if in real life you actually had to join or try to set up a dictatorship, you could end up in a remote jail, or assassinated! And I get the impression that Whitehead is big on the importance of taking risks of being wrong for the effectiveness of learning. I sense that somehow that is right, but I don't want to get off track here on that.

The thing I am after is that Harry's fear of failure as a motivation goes right against Whitehead, because it makes school too much like the outside world—make a mistake and horrible consequences could ensue. Good God. What an idea—it just struck me that that condemns most existing schools! I'd better go easy on Harry with this one, or he'll make a complete fool out of me—more than likely just at the moment the principal walks through the door. Excuse me, journal. Telephone's ringing.

I was only half listening to the patter of the carpet-cleaning company on the phone, and I suddenly wondered why I am keeping a journal. Well, I enjoy it, in some sense, anyway. But I'm sure it's more than that. It is. Somehow it's more helpful than just thinking, because you don't forget so easily what you said before, or get paralyzed trying to remember it. No, I've just had a marvelous idea: it's safer to first explore things you don't properly understand in a journal. I can take risks, be as stupid or optimistic as I like along the way, and there's no one to be judgmental—to laugh at it, or sneer at it, or completely misunderstand what I'm fumbling for. That fits beautifully with what I got from the Whitehead passage! Thanks Journal, but enough is enough, for the moment, anyway. For goodness sake, don't wake me at three in the morning with some profound insight!

### 7 October

I managed to get Harry in one place long enough to try some of these ideas on him. I ended up confused and depressed. He was skeptical and quite unmoved, and without having the book there I trailed off into vagueness. Nonetheless, he also didn't convince me of his position, but he did make an interesting point (which I feel somehow is wrong), and here I am, back with book and journal, and yet another idea I hadn't had before—so far as I can tell.

Harry said that it sounded to him as if Whitehead was rather typical of educational theorists who get lost in ideals, get out of touch with the daily reality of the classroom teacher, and dramatize fine-sounding notions which can't be followed in practice, however much we too would like some of them to be possible to follow. Later that day I realized why (although six months ago I would have agreed with him) I had a strong sense there is a serious problem with what he says. He seems to be implying at least two things. First, Whitehead's ideas are the sort which sound nice but are impossible to put into practice in our schools. Second, even if some of these ideas are completely correct, we should forget them because they would involve far too much difficulty and conflict in the system as it is now. Yes, reading over this, I'm sure these were the points he was making.

Let's deal with the first one first. (Am I finally getting the point about thought being disciplined?) Well, one idea I talked about was Whitehead's conviction, and mine, that you can't get the kind of learning that makes for a really good type of personal development unless the student finds the work itself to have a significant amount of personal interest. Why can't that be put into practice right now? The fact is that to some extent it is already taking place in this school and other schools, and I have many times succeeded in bringing it about for some students in a class. (Though I didn't have any clear reason for doing that. It just felt right.)

So much for that one. What about the idea that school learning is of the best kind if students are not afraid of making mistakes, that is, not afraid of being failed for getting the wrong answer, of being made to look a fool, and so on? I don't see that just because we have marks and exams and right answers, therefore we are forced to make them such a big deal that kids get frightened into working (or angered into not working). Why can't we take the same material that will be graded and find ways to make studying it of some personal interest? The answer is that we can—to some extent at least—and what is more I even personally know two teachers who seem very good at doing just that for much of the study time. So that one is answered as well. (Why couldn't I have said all this when I was talking to Harry?)

Then there was what I said to him about ideas shaping our lives, so that being careful with our ideas, and getting the best ideas, was necessary in education. He said certificates also shape our lives, and our first concern as teachers was to make sure the students get the certificates they need, and the School Board and Department of Education can worry over the curriculum. That really stopped me at the time, but now I think that although he's not wrong in every way, his argument is full of holes. I can't imagine how I swallowed it. Just imagine if Harry turned over page 98 of his curriculum guide and saw that he has to teach the kids that Marx is the only person worth reading if you want to understand history and what is happening with people today! Would Harry teach that? Not on your life! He'd be phoning the School Board, haranguing the principal, stirring up the teacher association, and goodness knows what else. What does all that mean, then? Surely it means that when we don't question the ideas of the curriculum it's only because at some level we have already decided they are all right. Unless we feel we simply can't judge and then we trust the judgment of the authorities in the area. What else could we do? A teacher, as a responsible professional, would not agree to teach what he or she thought was incorrect or horribly biased or plain destructive. If that's so, I think that I was right after all. It certainly is part of the teacher's job to evaluate the ideas being dealt with in the class, or, for that matter, to bring in important ideas that are not being dealt with, whether they are in the curriculum or not. And that means I can't just trot the ideas out from the book. I have to evaluate them to my own satisfaction, if I can. I don't mind that, since it makes most of the curriculum really interesting, and I like my job more. Harry, you are out to lunch on your first point, I'm afraid. No question that these ideas of Whitehead's can be put into practice immediately. What about the second? Well, maybe tomorrow. My brains have had enough for one day!

## 8 October

There could be trouble here, Journal! You are beginning to provoke jealousy. My wife says all this writing is beginning to get a bit much, and aren't I beginning to take things a little too seriously? I wasn't aware that spouses could be jealous of thinking. There's a lot I seem to be learning in cahoots with you!

Anyway, there's no stopping me today. I have found an intriguing passage in Whitehead's book which has taken me on a good deal from where I was yesterday. But, discipline! First things first. I still have a point of Harry's left over from yesterday.

Harry's second point was that even if some of Whitehead's ideas are right, forget them, because trying to put them into practice would unleash a mess of trouble (or words to that effect). But Whitehead is talking about education, so that if one of his ideas is right, it implies the right way to educate. In that case, to forget it and carry on doing something different—I mean, working with a different idea, would very likely be working with an idea which is not true to education, or may even work against educating. If that were so, we would have a school in which we do some things that are not educational—and I don't mean scrubbing the floor and eating lunch, either. I mean learning the wrong things, or learning in the wrong way, or something serious like that. This situation is beginning to look absurd—we have a school in which we are not going to do what it takes to educate kids, because that would be too difficult! So, following this argument along, we have a school in which we do what is easy and not educational, so as to be "practical" rather than idealistic dreamers. What self-respecting educator could buy that?

Now I've found something pretty interesting about ideals. At the beginning of Chapter Three in *The Aims* Whitehead says:

> The fading of ideals is sad evidence of the defeat of human endeavor. In the schools of antiquity philosophers aspired to impart wisdom, in modern colleges our humbler aim is to teach subjects. The drop from the divine wisdom . . . to text-book knowledge of subjects, marks an educational failure sustained through the ages. . . . My point is that, at the dawn of our European civilization, men started with the full ideals which should inspire education, and that gradually our ideals have sunk to square with our practice. . . . But when ideals have sunk to the level of practice, the result is stagnation . . . though there will be much activity, amid aimless rearrangement of syllabuses, in the fruitless endeavor to dodge the inevitable lack of time.

There's so much that interests me and that I'm not sure about in this passage now I've written it, I hardly know where to start or where I was going. Oh yes! One thing Whitehead is adamant about is the importance of having ideals, the right ideals. In addition (this is really interesting), the ideals have to be applied to reveal things we are not already doing, or not doing well enough. This is the way I understand it: the whole point about having ideals is that they always suggest something more and better than you are doing. That would mean that without such ideals you wouldn't have any motivation to improve or any way of judging that you are improving at all—rather than changing things around trivially or even for the worse. So taking ideals seriously is not necessarily to be impractical or a useless dreamer. In fact, it seems stronger than that. Let's see if I can get it into words. What I see now is that in some way one would be stupid not to have ideals—one wouldn't be "practical." Because if I am a responsible professional educator, part of my responsibility is to keep improving my practice (since it always falls short somewhere), and if improvement relies on ideals, I can't be anything but irresponsible and rather stupid if I try to be "practical" without ideals. Phew! My reasoning is getting a bit convoluted. But going through it again I'm sure it is okay, and that I'm right on this one. No wonder Whitehead spends the whole of the first page of a chapter on this topic; maybe he should have made it the first whole page of the book! Come to think of it, my skipping about in the book as my fancy takes me is perhaps going too far, because I realize I haven't even read the first page! But maybe that's enough for this evening, or there could be a row brewing in this usually peaceful establishment!

## 12 October

Having read over the last two entries, I realize I have so many questions it's difficult to know where I want to start here. I have mixed feelings about Whitehead's emphasis on "wisdom" as the proper ideal for education. Or should I call it the central or most important ideal? I'd guess the latter. Wisdom sounds important, but somehow out of place for school education—at least as I know it. Perhaps I am simply habituated to aim for lesser things. Can children be taught so they become wise? Wouldn't that need a teacher who has wisdom, or who at least regards it as crucial? I certainly don't think of myself as wise, and I can only think of a handful of adults I have met who strike me as probably having wisdom. Come to think of it, I'm not sure I even know what wisdom is! (I wonder why we didn't have to ponder these things during teacher education?)

The other thing bothering me is that I see I have been jumping from "ideas" to "ideals" and back again without a thought about whether that is a muddle or not. I started thinking about ideas as what we think with, and then just moved on to thinking with ideals. I have to try to sort out the difference before I go on. Where does one start? Well, let's try, "Are they the same?" They seem to be, since they are both things we think with, so as to affect how we live, how we act. Hitler and Gandhi are obviously men with big ideas, but for each man, all the ideas somehow seem to be held together as an ideal. How? It looks as though an ideal is a special kind of idea. Yes, I feel sure about that. But what kind? My guess at the moment is this: an ideal is a special kind of idea which gives one some definite and passionate purpose. It also seems to indicate what we think would be best to aim at achieving—not for little things, but for things to do with what one's whole life serves. Ideas, simply as ideas, don't seem to be like that. I mean, for example, I have an idea that a Porsche is a "car," and I have an idea of what a "car" is. I also have an idea that a Porsche is on most counts a better car than a Volkswagen Beetle. But neither of these ideas is anything I really care about, and neither of them makes me want to gather up my whole life and head in a special direction. All right, let's say then that we can have any number of ideas, but only some of them will become ideals for us. I've thought of a better way of saying that: some of our ideas become very big and special to us, giving life a special concern or meaning; these ideas are our ideals.

Now I want to get back on the ground again! I know there are a lot of ideas about what, overall, teachers should aim at for their students, like: good jobs, thinking well, a lot of knowledge, wisdom, and so on. Each teacher could select one or two of these as his or her personal ideals for education. That brings me back to Whitehead. What does he mean by "wisdom," and is it really the most important or central or overall idea for education, such that I ought to have it as my central ideal? How would that affect, for example, teaching grade five kids long division or the history of Canada?

I wanted to just skim over those problems and get to the first page of Whitehead's book, which I have now read, because he has some notion of an "inert" idea which he thinks is the biggest problem for all education. But that will have to wait; I feel mentally burned out at the moment.

### 14  October

I found myself alone in the staff room with Glenda, the grade four teacher. Harry must have spoken to her about our conversations because she said, "Been giving Harry a hard time lately, have you? Good for you! Not many can stand up to his forceful views—even when they don't amount to very much. He comes on as a slightly superior pragmatist, but really he's a despairing idealist, don't you think?"

Really I hadn't thought about a label for Harry—I was focusing more on what he was saying. The notion of wisdom was on my mind, and I seized the opportunity to ask her what she thought. She played around a bit, made fun of my question, but then got quite thoughtful and quiet.

She said, "Well, one of the few things I remember from a philosophy class at university was being struck by the Socratic idea that the first step in wisdom is realizing you don't know. I remember how in one of Plato's dialogues, the *Meno,* Socrates examines the theories of virtue put forth by an arrogant intellectual, Meno, and finds them all inadequate. I mean, he destroys every one of them systematically, utterly, leaving Meno with nothing. The professor said that for Socrates it was clear you can't begin to really discover what is true until you realize that you don't know. Then you naturally begin to look seriously, instead of playing with attractive little theories you've picked up here and there, ready-made."

I was impressed. I'd never spoken seriously to Glenda before. Later, I remembered reading that Socrates thought to "know thyself" was somehow quite fundamental. And I can see that knowing you yourself don't know is knowing something about yourself.

The trouble is, although I like that idea as the beginning of wisdom, I'm still left in the dark about what wisdom is if you get it after beginning that way. I must stop here. I'll comfort myself with the thought that at least I know I don't know what wisdom is!

## 17 October

I've been looking at that page in *The Aims* about ideals and wisdom again. Initially, I thought Whitehead was running down "text-book knowledge" and knowledge of "subjects." After reading the first page of the book (and a bit more), I think he's only bothered about ideas when they become "inert ideas" for the student. He says inert ideas are "ideas that are merely received into the mind without being utilized, or tested, or thrown into fresh combinations." That almost seems to mean just memorizing someone else's words, beliefs, techniques, skills—whatever—without any real understanding. Then you could say them but not use them in your life, or show why you thought them true or important. Or perhaps you could use them only in the way you learned them, but not when they are needed in some different kind of situation. I have to admit that does sound like an inferior kind of learning, and I'm sure too much of my schooling (and teacher education) was like that. So if "teaching subjects" (rather than progressing toward wisdom) results in these inert ideas, it's worse than a "drop from the divine wisdom to text-book knowledge." It's a complete waste of everyone's time!

Reading over, I see I lost something. My point is, I don't think subject-teaching has to result in inert ideas, and it shouldn't, but too often in fact it does.

Why on earth didn't I read on from that passage on wisdom and ideals! On the very next page Whitehead starts explaining what he means by wisdom. He isn't against subject-teaching as such, because he says, "knowledge is one chief aim of education." Good that he isn't against it, since he was a subject-teacher himself! In math. In fact I saw somewhere that he himself wrote a little book on math that's good for teachers—*An Introduction to Mathematics.*

Now this is more like it. Whitehead says wisdom is to do with the way we "handle" knowledge, how we use knowledge to "determine relevant issues," and "to add value to our immediate experience." I think he means all this together, not one or the other.

Then Whitehead says you can't impart wisdom by "spouting" at the students. The "only avenue" is by "freedom in the presence of knowledge." Freedom in the presence of knowledge? That doesn't click for me. What kind of freedom? To go back, Hitler felt free to use all sorts of knowledge as he thought fit, and he certainly was not wise. Gandhi I admire—even more so after that wonderful movie. Why was he wise? Well, he knew how to get the people to use their knowledge and skills to become self-sufficient, rather than pathetically dependent. He also knew that violence only breeds more violence, and resolutely stuck to peaceful means.

I remember a story about Gandhi. A mother brought her child to Gandhi and asked him to stop the boy eating candies all the time. Gandhi told her to bring him back next week. When she did so, he told the boy to stop eating candies because they would ruin his health. The mother asked why he had waited a week just to say that. Gandhi replied that he also was addicted to candies and needed a week to give them up himself first. That's wise, I think. But why? Perhaps it's because he knew that you can't persuade others to improve themselves unless you really have the knowledge that it can be done by having done it yourself. That's what is called "truth felt on the pulse," I suppose. What is that? The truth of an idea tested in your life? (That would not be inert.) Seeing for yourself that an idea is true? (I don't emphasize that enough in my class.)

How does all this connect with Whitehead's statements about wisdom? Does it connect at all? Well, time for a bit of truly disciplined thought. Let's take "the way knowledge is handled." The wise use their knowledge to sort out with great care what the "relevant issues" are. Okay, if I apply that to Gandhi I would say he used his knowledge of people, himself, law, and so on, to see that a relevant (I'd say crucial) issue is that of people attaining a sense of usefulness, skill, with freedom and dignity (self-respect), but not by violent means. How many people see that with such clarity when it comes to action? Not many.

The other criterion of wisdom, Whitehead says, is the employment of knowledge to add value to our immediate experience. I sense that by "value," here, he implies beneficial value. I don't think Hitler (amongst others!) could pass on that one! Could Gandhi? No question that he did. Under his influence (at least for a while) the people came to feel their lives as much more valuable, worthwhile, vital—however you want to express it. (I meant not simply his, but the influence of his knowledge, and then their own.)

I see I've forgotten the story of the boy eating too many candies. How does that fit as wisdom? One thing he realized is that if your life doesn't reflect your words (and vice versa?), then you can't influence others even to do something merely sensible. Perhaps your own, and their, sense of yourself as a hypocrite blocks their willingness to consider what you have to say. What criterion of Whitehead's does that illustrate? I think it must have to do with the way you "handle" knowledge—so that it affects your life and isn't just a theory floating around in the mind. But there's also a special insight into people here, and a real respect for them. I've heard of people with special gifts who use them to harm others, so that respecting people, wanting what is good for them, seems essential in this matter of wisdom. I can't make sense of "wisdom" as a gift of using special knowledge and powers to harm or exploit others. That strikes me as absurd. I don't think Whitehead deals with that clearly, and I think he should. It's sort of in-between the lines, but it ought to be right out in the open.

Well, thanks, Journal, I feel we've got somewhere tonight.

## 18 October

I have to leave for school, but I had an idea in bed before going to sleep, and I want to get it down before I forget it. I remembered that I once read a story somewhere about the Buddha, and I remember it precisely because he struck me as extremely wise.

As I remember it, a woman came to the Buddha complaining and lamenting about the death of her child, and blaming God (or Brahma, or Fate, whatever it was) for selecting her to suffer in this way. The Buddha told her to go to every house in the village and collect for him the names of all those families who had not suffered such a tragedy. She did so, and returned. The Buddha asked for the names. She told him there weren't any to give him— every household had suffered a similar tragedy. I don't think, in the story, he said anything to that. She got the point herself.

Why does that strike me as wise? Well, he had obviously realized, as she hadn't, that everyone suffers to some degree, and basically in very similar ways. But he didn't use this knowledge to tell her, to give her a lecture on The Rules of the Universe! For sure she wouldn't have listened in her angry state, or it would have been merely pious words to her, affecting nothing. No, the Buddha sent her off to discover that truth for herself. Then she felt the weight of it, she was helped by it (even if her child didn't come back to life). I can see a lot more here, too, though whether it was in the Buddha's mind I don't know. When she went round the village, she almost certainly got some support and sympathy from many and probably was "taken out of herself" (her pain and anger) by sympathy for the loss others had experienced—much of it undoubtedly greater than hers.

I sense a lot of things here for education that is wise, like working together on things, finding out for oneself (even if others help), sharing, etc.

## 20 October

I don't want to write any more on wisdom for the moment. I can't see how to go further, and I'm a bit tired of the topic.

Thinking through Whitehead's *Aims of Education*, I'm not getting inspired at the moment—I'm getting paralyzed! There are so many interesting ideas, so many qualifications of them, embellishments, connections to other topics, etc., that I'm bewildered. I can't see it all as a whole and can't see exactly where I could start in my class to use it. I can play (and have been playing) around with bits and pieces, but I sense that if I could see it all as a whole I would be much surer what to change and why. This bewilderment just makes me tired. I've no energy for thinking tonight. Well, dear Journal, perhaps you've come to the end of your usefulness.

Wait a minute! Just as I closed the journal and got up to make a phone call, I had an inspiration. If wisdom, or part of it, is working together, I wonder if it would be better to explore some of this with a group of interested people? But who? I don't know. I'll ask Glenda tomorrow what she thinks. A problem might be that if we're all new to Whitehead we might just get more and more muddled. Well, we'll see. If it is wise to work together on things, perhaps we should check that out by doing it. I feel I'm beginning to burble—that is enough for tonight.

### 21 October

Glenda was at least interested in the idea of a discussion group. But she didn't hold out much hope for enough interested teachers in the school. She was right. I stopped everyone I could and put the idea to them. "Too busy"; "Want to get away from education in my spare time, not into it again"; "We are doing all right in the school already, so why look for new ideas?" "Who's Whitehead?" And so it went on. It thoroughly depressed me. But Maria, the kindergarten teacher, was quite excited, and made a good suggestion. Apparently she is in an evening course at the University Faculty of Extension—one of these personal interest courses without credit—and has a professor from the department of Educational Foundations. She is quite taken with his approach and says he has several times quoted Whitehead, but she doesn't know if it is the same one. Anyway she is going to ask him if he has any ideas about a discussion group and how to get interested people involved. She said there was a man, Frank, in her class (about the history of educational ideas, I think) who she was sure would be interested.

### 23 October

My wife's ill with flu and our dinner date is off, so I might as well do some writing—though I don't have any great ideas. I'm impatient to see what comes of Maria's inquiries.

Werner, the computer enthusiast on our staff, was reading a book by Roszak—*The Cult of Information*. Theodore Roszak, I think. Going over a few pages I got quite hooked, especially when I sensed he is saying something similar to Whitehead—in a way. Roszak says that exaggerating the power of computers by excitable technicians and profiteering companies is getting teachers muddled about the difference between information and ideas, and the difference between information processing and thinking. He says information is facts, but thinking needs ideas to get anything significant out of the facts. So ideas are not the same as facts or information. He thinks we have confused information and ideas in education, and that's why we tend to get students to remember a lot of facts, like a computer storing information, rather than teaching thinking. As I see it, Whitehead would say those merely remembered facts become inert ideas for the students, because they don't do enough thinking about them. I'd say that in education we need facts, but more importantly we need to teach students how to use ideas to make something out of, or with, facts. (Roszak also says we don't have any facts without ideas. That's a curious notion and I'm not sure what he means.)

I've lost something somewhere. Oh, yes. Roszak goes further and says that as long as we insist that computers really think, and take them as a model for thinking, we are in danger of strengthening the old idea of education as filling up with facts. That's it. Now I remember. He says that information processing is not the same as thinking, and that the closest it comes to thinking is that it connects facts logically—rather like the mathematician connecting numbers logically—but that all this relies on the ideas the programmer builds into the program in the first place. Also, that whatever we do with the connected facts, or the connections of the facts (both, I suppose) depends on what ideas we have to work with. And, as I remember, he says something like: the important job in serious thinking is finding out what ideas we are working with, and looking at them critically, and that computers can help us little in this, and certainly don't do this themselves.

So what I get from this is that you can only do a very limited type of thinking using computers, and if you confuse that with thinking in all its varieties, as a teacher you will tend to drastically limit the kinds of thinking you encourage, and so impoverish the students' minds. To me, this means, for example, that a student could "learn" (be told, believe, and remember) the fact that there was a Russian revolution in the early twentieth century, and the fact that Lenin was a kind of Marxist, but never learn to think out whether Lenin's ideas were good ones or not, or if the revolution really improved the lives of Russians, and so on. So then students are like computers storing facts which can be "processed," or connected logically in certain ways (Lenin came after, not before Marx, for example), but apart from that they can do nothing significant with the facts, so far as their own lives are concerned. Because they can't really think. The information is inert. Intelligence is inert. Come to

think of it, the student would then be a bit like a machine. I wonder if Whitehead ever said this?

Another thought! Such a student, as child or adult, would be as easily
persuaded by a communist propagandist as by a capitalist! I wonder if the Russians (or Chinese or Cubans) really teach their students to think? That could
be dangerous to the firm commitment to a communist way of life. For that
matter, it was dangerous to the Russian student—Solzhenitsyn certainly found
that out, the Siberian way! That gives me another idea: real thinking can be
risky for any individual or state. So if I am going to say that education primarily has to do with real thinking, I have to accept that education can be a risky
business for the status quo. That's interesting—I always thought of education
as a pretty stabilizing, conservative, useful but harmless activity. Real thinking is obviously good for freedom, but it could get one into trouble with
family, church, even the state itself—one could end up in jail, perhaps.
"Education leads to jail!" That's excessive, I'm sure, but I couldn't resist it as
a provocation. It somehow challenges this stodgy notion of schooling being
essential to success and security. Learning to spell is essential in that way,
probably, but learning to think critically about the wisdom of democracy could
land one on the street in Europe and North America.

Well, that's it, dear Journal, for what it's worth. Now to see what Maria
turns up on Monday.

(Looking back over this, I'm not sure I know what I'm talking about
when I say "real" thinking. Oh well, another time.)

## 26 October

Good news, Journal. Maria came through with flying colors. She came to find
me in the morning recess to tell me that she spoke to her professor. Not only
is he interested in the suggestion, but he is willing, should the group desire it,
to coordinate it—because he enjoys Whitehead. Professor Freedman doesn't
claim to be an expert on Whitehead's ideas (though, according to Maria, he
doesn't like being called an expert in anything!), but he regularly includes
Whitehead's ideas in his teaching in philosophy of education, and would wel-
come the chance to discuss them in a concentrated way to get a better hold on
them himself. He also suggested we do something thorough with just one
book we have all read. He said *The Aims of Education and Other Essays* is the
obvious choice.

When Maria raised the question of participants, he agreed to pass the
word around his own classes and colleagues, and invited her to announce the
discussion group in that class herself at the next meeting. I feel sure we will
get enough people to get it started. Perhaps too many! Maria and I will have

to discuss that, too. Professor Freedman suggested that meeting at someone's home might give the participants a sense of comfort, and eliminate some of the feeling of constraint attached to institutionalized learning. Of course I immediately said that my home was available. The large living room could hold quite a few people. The part-time music teacher, Jerry Lovett, heard us talking about it, and said he would like to try it. He said he once read a book of Whitehead's on science, called *Science and the Modern World*, and found it impossible to put down. Although he didn't know Whitehead had written anything on education, he said he felt sure it would be worth reading and talking about.

Maria is really practical. She even thought to ask Professor Freedman how much time he could spare, and apparently he is willing to give an evening every two or three weeks to it for two or three months, but that need not limit the group.

Now we wait to see if we get any more people interested.

Harry heard about it through the grapevine (he wasn't in school when I asked around). He made the expected cracks about the idea, like, "I hear you are arranging a dream interpretation class, Ryan." Well, I suppose if any dream can survive his skeptical and cynical comments, it is pretty sure to be more than a dream, so I'll try to think of him positively as the acid which will show what is gold by dissolving everything else! That should suit him, since he poses as such a scientific realist.

## 28 October

Now the process is started, I'm really impatient to hear whether Maria can get some interested people from her class, or elsewhere, for the discussion group. Glenda is fairly enthusiastic. She said she could do with some intelligent conversation for a change. She added that it would be good to have some practicing teachers, but thought a few people from other walks of life might stop the discussions from getting too narrow and "incestuous." Maria's class is not until tomorrow night, so I just have to sit on my impatience for the moment.

Perhaps in the meantime I could get somewhere with that unresolved thought from last week: what do I mean when I refer to "real" thinking? It's curious how I do know that I mean something definite, and yet at this point can't put it satisfactorily into words. Nor do I know where to start to find out how to say it, but I am beginning to feel more confident that if I mess around for a while something clear will emerge. Testing. . . .

Got it! I knew that for some reason what happened in class today was quite important. Jamie, who is famed for being annoying, has shown another side of himself, and it makes me wonder if we haven't been getting annoyed at intelligence without realizing it! A fine state of affairs if teachers get annoyed at intelligence! We were in math class, and I asked if there were any questions before they worked over some examples. Jamie asked if they could all have a lesson in ESP, so that they could simply tune in to my math knowledge and get all the answers right. I could feel my annoyance rising in the certainty that all the class would now be distracted, but then I realized that he wasn't simply being an idiot, and many of the kids were struck silent and interested in the idea. So I did something different. I asked how many would like to hear Jamie explain his idea. I was drowned in a sea of hands, and when they quieted down Jamie explained quite seriously and lucidly that his sister in high school had read a magazine article which said that Australian aborigines could contact each other from one side of the continent to the other by ESP. And if they can do it—seeing what's in each other's mind—why can't we?

I was stumped as to what to say, so I unwittingly did what I think was a good thing anyway and asked if anyone wanted to comment. A usually quiet and shy girl, Sarah, spoke up immediately and quite boldly, without any of her usual self-consciousness, and I became quite intrigued. She recounted how she had watched a film on TV about Kalahari Bushmen in Africa, and the commentator had remarked that they could send messages across hundreds of miles to each other in an instant, and the message is felt by the receiver at first as what they call a "tapping" in the chest. She said they could also get messages in the same way about the future. (Who on earth would send those?) It just struck me that our instant relay of information via computers and satellites is rather primitive if what the kids were saying is true. Anyway, a thoroughly serious discussion started up spontaneously in the class, with pretty good order, and the questions they were asking floored me with their ingenuity. One girl asked, "What if you could do this ESP sending, but you had some private thoughts you wanted to keep to yourself? How would you stop them going to someone else?" By allowing ten minutes for that spontaneous conversation—and not accusing Jamie of disruption with comments irrelevant to math—I discovered a completely new side to the students' capabilities, and they had a good experience of real thinking. There it is again, "real" thinking. That's what I wanted to clarify for myself.

Why was this real thinking? Well, let's see. The kind of thinking they were doing in the math—understanding a rule and applying it in some test examples—is real thinking in the sense that some kind of thinking is really going on. But it isn't the same kind of thinking that was going on in the spontaneous discussion. In math, the thinking was sort of mechanical, programmed—you have a rule, you apply it. But in the discussion of ESP there were no rules like that to work with. In fact, they had to discover if there were any rules to understanding ESP, so it was quite creative. Also, it was extremely animated; there was a spark (and sparkle) to it that was quite absent in their learning to do the math. It had an immediate personal interest for them, or most of them, and carried the sense of something excitingly new—a modification of the way they (and I) see the world, and the sense of a new mental possibility opening to them. It was about being able to communicate in difficult circumstances and about guarding their privacy if they so wished. I guess they don't have any similarly interesting sense of the immediate relevance of the math to themselves.

I wonder if there is a way to do the math so that it does carry some kind of immediate personal interest for them? I hope so, partly because I do think it is important for them to know some of this basic math, though how much of it is basic I'm not sure. I remember a passage in Whitehead's *Aims* I noticed yesterday, and in it he seems to be expressing just this kind of question. On page 32 he says:

> The environment within which the mind is working must be carefully selected. It must, of course, be chosen to suit the child's stage of growth, and must be adapted to individual needs. In a sense it is an imposition from without; but in a deeper sense it answers to the call of life within the child. In the teacher's consciousness the child has been sent to his telescope to look at the stars, in the child's consciousness he has been given free access to the glory of the heavens.

The work has to be done, but the art of teaching is the issue, and it entails finding out how to present it to the students so that it seems just the thing they want to do right now, or at least so it has interest in their present stage of life. And I can see that Whitehead implies that the significance for the student, if this is achieved, is what the learning opens up freshly to him. There is no motivation by a reward other than that enjoyment of the learning itself. That's how it was with the children discussing ESP. There was no reward for the use of their intelligence other than the fascination the subject seemed to have for them at the time. The question is, how on earth would I do that for even some of them in that piece of math learning? At the moment I just don't know. Nonetheless, it's now on my mind, so I might get an inspiration. There wouldn't have been much possibility for that if I hadn't hit on the question and taken it seriously.

I've just seen something else. A few lines further on, Whitehead says that "education is not a process of packing articles in a trunk." Now that, surely, is what I was reading in the Roszak book, about the mistake of thinking of the learning mind in the way one thinks of computers storing and processing information. That is like a sophisticated kind of "packing articles in a trunk." Whitehead wrote this somewhere around 1920. We seem to take an awfully long time to cotton on to some of these basic necessary ideas in education. Or maybe I should be saying, in schools, because I am getting an uncomfortable feeling that a great deal of what we do so seriously in school is not educational in its effect. Come to think of it, I'm not really sure how much of it is even educational in its intent. Now that's a thought for you, no, for me. I almost forget it's me doing the thinking here, by myself. This journal is beginning to feel like a contributing partner in a dialogue!

## 30 October

Glenda, I mean Maria, has got two people in her class interested, and Professor Freedman has another two. At first I felt disappointed, but then I realized that we already then have Glenda, Jerry, possibly my wife, Lou (Louise), Maria, Professor Freedman (Henry, I think), myself, and four others. That's eleven. That could even be too many. Perhaps we'll have to wait so long to get a word in edgeways we'll get really frustrated. I wonder also if Professor Freedman properly understands that we don't want to be lectured at. It sounds as if he does, but I don't know if Maria was completely clear on that with him.

Maria and Freedman have even set a tentative starting date and meeting place: at my house! At first I thought that a bit presumptuous, but now I think I was being petty. They were just enthusiastic to get started, not thoughtless or rude. So there it is: Sunday, the fifth of November, at six in the evening, for our first meeting, and it looks as if most can make it. Freedman and Maria still have to phone two people to check.

My project for spare time on the weekend will be to try to do at least a quick reading of the whole of *The Aims*—except perhaps the last three chapters, which look philosophically out of my depth and not obviously connected with the rest. Unless perhaps they are examples of the problems we have in trying to make sense of the world—in which case I imagine something of educational significance might well come from them. Freedman might have something on this.

## 31 October

Everyone is contacted now and has replied definitely one way or the other. The number coming is less than we predicted, but more manageable for a good discussion group, I think. As I see it, we need enough people to ensure a fair diversity of attitudes, experience and thinking, but few enough to allow each person to have plenty of space to speak his or her mind with some completeness. At the moment the list looks good—small and quite well balanced. We have:

David Ryan
Louise Ryan (Lou is now definite that she wants to be in on this)
Maria Vanzelli—kindergarten teacher
Glenda Martin—grade four teacher
Jerry Lovett—music specialist teacher
Craig Stonehouse—fourth year undergraduate B.Ed. student, secondary science teaching major
Anne MacLean—graduate M.Ed. student, presently writing her thesis in the area of philosophy of education
(Craig and Anne were invited by Freedman)
Frank Lederer—high school math teacher (invited from the University Extension Department "Education" class, friend of Maria)
Henry Freedman

So that's nine. And tomorrow we'll see how the personalities go together. I realize I'm anxious for this to work. I must just plan and relax and let it go as it will.

# PART 2
## The Dialogues

# Two

# THE PARTICIPANTS

**David Ryan**—organizer of the group, and introduced through his journal entries.

**Louise Ryan**—wife of David.

Louise is a good-humored housewife, former legal secretary, and affectionate mother of two. She is familiar with, not perturbed by, and still able to be curious about David's periodic bursts of enthusiasm to go deeper into something. The children are in elementary school, and her growing dissatisfaction with the school system and some of the teachers in her children's school is part of her motivation to hear what the group has to say. Her educational orientation is roughly that of a concerned parent who still sees schooling uncritically as a useful socialization process, not without flaws, but necessary to her children's ability to cope and to thrive in the society as it is. She does not question the general direction and structure of the school system as such but is beginning, through maternal concern, to have doubts on "humanistic" grounds. She is becoming active as a parent in the school her children attend and would like to feel more confident in a well-grounded stand of her own from which she can better argue what are intuitions regarding the way her children should be treated in school.

**Maria Vanzelli**—the kindergarten teacher in the same school as David.

Maria is an energetic, practical, emotionally expressive woman, warm and considerate with the young children in her care. She had been secure in her belief in a set of vague but sensible-sounding "early childhood education" principles and is still resourceful in the kind of practices which she associates with them and to which she was introduced in her teacher education. Three years as a professional teacher in the school system have cracked her assurance badly at points, and she has therefore seized eagerly on the group as an opportunity to find a more solid background system of beliefs for what she does as a teacher. Her attitude toward young children is of natural enjoyment, protective, and sentimental. The sentimentality is crumbling dangerously in the face of experience with many children and the quite different views of them in the minds of adults who often influence what she can and cannot do in her work.

**Glenda Martin**—the grade four teacher in the same school as David and Maria.

Glenda is energetic and reliable in practical matters, but quite uncoordinated in her basic understanding of her life and her profession. Her thinking is always skipping enthusiastically from one idea to the next. She loses the thread of thought by getting lost in anecdotes suggested by any discussion she has. She is periodically disturbed to discover that two ideas she has comfortably held and championed side-by-side for months or years are contradictory. Although she used to be comfortable with this "butterfly" mental existence and even flaunted it in the face of those she regarded as "over-serious," she is becoming increasingly upset by the feeling that it is immature and silly. She is hoping, though she could not articulate this, that the group discussions will be a way for her quietly and without embarrassment to find or put together a broad and consistent basis of ideas defensible and admirable enough to give a powerful boost to her failing confidence in the face of thoughtful or tough-minded people.

**Jerry Lovett**—the specialist music teacher who has been running the school's music program through two mornings and an afternoon each week for four years.

Although Jerry still does not realize it, he is known by the students, with humor and some affection, as the "space-cadet," on account of his continuous romance with beautiful ideas that carry him away into a stunning mental countryside and have no obvious connection with his or anyone else's life. But he is fair, accommodating, and interesting, and his considerable skill on a number of musical instruments commands natural respect. If he were able to clarify what is really motivating him, he would have to admit that he is drawn to the idea of the discussion group in the hope of a pleasurable flight in the clouds of intellectual speculation. Curiously, that the world does not live up to his favorite ideals has never struck him as problematic. He remains tolerant and good-humored in the space of freedom accorded him in his work. As yet, no significant life crisis has overtaken him to shake his foundations and impress upon him the need to bring his thinking and his experience together into an understanding which illuminates and gives solid direction in the vicissitudes of day-to-day life.

**Craig Stonehouse**—fourth year undergraduate secondary science student majoring in the Faculty of Education teacher education program, some eight months away from his B.Ed. graduation.

Craig has a good intellect which he habitually uses to calculate what he needs to do to be successful. In his education studies, he leans toward the attitude of "no-nonsense, just find the right methods, stop talking and get on with the job." His self-confidence and strong personality have given him fair success on his practicum in keeping good order and firm direction in class. His supervisor and cooperating teacher were impressed and allowed him to interpret this as meaning he is a natural teacher. However, in his Educational Foundations philosophy of education class with Professor Freedman, some films of alternative approaches to education are giving him serious doubts about what he is doing. He hopes the discussion group with experienced teachers will give him a way of arguing to his own satisfaction that the approach he is comfortable with and good at is the correct one. His pragmatism also suggests to him that listening to them will make him appear unusually mature in his coming job interviews. Mingled with this is a genuine ethical sense of responsibility and a desire to do beneficial work in the world. This is what remains after his rejection of the outward trappings and explicit theology of his fundamentalist religious upbringing.

**Anne MacLean**—a graduate Educational Foundations student, presently writing her Philosophy of Education masters thesis, with Professor Freedman as one of her thesis committee advisors.

Although more sophisticated in abstract thinking and better informed than David about philosophy of education as a field of scholarly endeavor, Anne shares his unusual tenacity in thinking through issues and his strong sense of the logical connection of ideas. They both have a good balance in keeping their feet firmly on the ground while their heads peer freely around in higher atmospheres. She has experienced a dialogic approach to learning with Professor Freedman, handles it well, and feels the benefit of it. For this reason, and because her required course work is long finished, the discussion group offers her a way to keep in active touch with people of similar interests, as a contrast with the isolated work of preparing a theoretical dissertation.

**Frank Lederer**—a high school math teacher in the Faculty of Extension Education class with Maria.

This class is perhaps Frank's last hope that thinking might eventually give some convincing results to ease the burden of his cynicism, growing slowly, cancer-like, over the natural vitality of his spirit. He has become a careless teacher as conviction drains away, and he tries to compensate for this with an unpleasant and disliked authoritarianism in his teaching. He was not always like this. He is still made uncomfortable by those with dedication and vitality around him, and he still hopes that by some happy circumstance he might again be energized with conviction, patience, and some joy in the face of what he feels is an irredeemably ugly world. Rather like opposite poles of a magnet, he is drawn to Maria's passion, hope, and willingness to believe, and this attraction forms a strong part of his participation in the group discussion. She, on the other hand, while disliking Frank's cynical acquiescence, is drawn to him as a balance for her tendency to ride on waves of enthusiastic but uncritical acceptance. One ground of Frank's continuing spark of hope that he is wrong about life is Freedman himself. Frank cannot but acknowledge that Freedman is an older and more experienced man, amply aware of the imperfection of things and having a more acute mind than his own. Yet Freedman is not cynical, not a dreamer, not a fanatic, and not a self-centered pragmatist. He is quick to acknowledge what others have not recognized is beautiful or good, and equally realistic about what is ugly and tragic. So what is he? What is this sense of Freedman's stability and quietly constructive energy which he cannot identify and label? The question keeps Frank going and looking, for the time being.

# Three

# FIRST DIALOGUE:
# SHOULD A TEACHER TELL?

## Sunday, 5 November

Members of the group have arrived at David and Louise's house in time for an early dinner. After about an hour of informal chatting and eating cold meats and salads prepared by Louise and David, David brings in coffee, tea, juice, and cups and glasses. He looks pointedly at Professor Freedman as he puts them down, and Freedman gets up according to their arrangement and ambles over to one corner of the room. The others sense a change, and conversation slows to a gradual halt. David looks around and then speaks.

DAVID: Now you have had something to eat, please help yourselves to what-ever you want to drink.
MARIA: No wine, David?
GLENDA: At the *Symposium* dinner party, even Socrates drank wine with the rest.
LOUISE: Well, you have a point. It never occurred to us. Let's get some for next time.
FRANK: (*sarcastically*) I'm sure the intoxication of high ideas will be all we need.
MARIA: All right, all right, cut the sarcasm, Frank, I wasn't being that seri-ous. But it would be a nice idea for the future.
DAVID: I agree. When you have what you want to drink, please sit around in a circle—there are cushions if you would like to sit on the rug—over here with Professor Freedman. (*Everyone shuffles about finding a spot that suits him or her, the activity dies down, everyone seems comfortable, and attention shifts to Professor Freedman.*)
HENRY: Please don't call me "Professor Freedman." No one calls me that in my classes at the university, and it's even more out of place here since I'm not, in the usual sense, the teacher in this gathering. As I understand it, I have been asked to guide and focus our discussions for as long as it seems fruitful and necessary for someone in particular to do that. I don't see why as we go along others shouldn't take that position, or perhaps no one in that role will be necessary. Other than probably having more experience at that kind of thing, I am one of the participants, also here, like you, for what I can get out

of it for my own understanding. So please call me Henry, and don't offend me by abbreviating that to Hen! (*laughter*)

I think the inspiration for focusing on Whitehead is largely David's, but I have found Whitehead immensely useful over the years. He's still telling me things I don't know and need to. His schema for the proper progress of learning through "romance," "precision," and "generalization" stages has gradually come to be an ever-present force in my thinking at the practical level of organizing my own teaching, and I still can't see how to apply the schema consistently over every part of my teaching. That doesn't imply that the schema is hopelessly vague, but that it is very rich in continually novel possibilities and is an unending source of challenge to the imagination in teaching. To put it simply, it is one of the most potent sources of my staying alive as a practicing educator. You don't necessarily need the schema as a teacher, but you certainly do, I would say, as an educator.

CRAIG: I don't understand that. Teacher, educator? What's the difference?

HENRY: Good question, though I think it's a bit premature to go into that now. Can we settle for a promise to get to it eventually?

CRAIG: That's fine.

HENRY: All right. Now it also makes sense to look carefully at Whitehead. Not only was he one of the century's finest thinkers, though poorly known in education circles, and philosophical ones for that matter, but also he was always conscious of his degree of effectiveness as an educator and concerned about education in general. He served on some important educational committees in England and was an important force in putting the London polytechnics on the map. But I don't see why we should confine ourselves exclusively to Whitehead; there are other fine thinkers in the field with some interestingly similar and contrasting views. It could be helpful to bring them in where they naturally fit. This will help Whitehead's ideas become clearer. That's just a suggestion, I mean, if you want to bring in Mohammed, fine—it's your group.

GLENDA: (*puzzled*) I've never heard of Mohammed in education. (*laughter*)

DAVID: Glenda, I think Henry was just cracking a joke.

HENRY: I was, but come to think of it, I have a vague memory that he did stipulate some things about education that I would be very much opposed to—or perhaps it was others in Islam, building on his influence.

GLENDA: Thanks for bailing me out!

HENRY: Well, I'm serious. But what I wanted to get around to is whether everyone has some familiarity with Whitehead's educational writings. Has anyone read *The Aims* all the way through? (*A chorus of voices saying different things breaks out.*)

HENRY: Let's take it one by one then. David?

DAVID: Just a surface read of all but the last three chapters. I dipped into them and they looked very difficult, and I don't see how they fit into the book.
HENRY: "The Organization of Thought" and "The Anatomy of Some Scientific Ideas" would seem to have some relevance to educators in general and to science and mathematics teachers in particular. Craig and Frank might find them quite interesting. "Space, Time, and Relativity"—well, again Craig and Frank come to mind. We might find that something very important related to the more obvious educational themes of the book is worked out in those chapters. My sense is that we will have our hands full with the first seven chapters, and in them the educational reference is explicit. Has anyone else read the first seven chapters?
MARIA and ANNE: Yes.
HENRY: Has anyone not yet read any of it? (*silence*) Has anyone not managed to get hold of a copy of their own?
JERRY: I'm using a library copy, but I haven't even tried a bookstore yet. I'll do that next week, because I like to mark up my books as I read them. I gather from people here that it's not difficult to get hold of a copy.
HENRY: Then it would probably work best if we raise some of our general questions about education this evening. If we get some of those fairly clear, your reading of Whitehead will probably have more impact. Then in the meantime everyone could do at least a once-through of the first seven chapters, and jot some questions down to bring to our next session. How does that sound? (*A chorus of agreement resounds.*)
MARIA: I don't understand why, if you're familiar with Whitehead's ideas, you don't give us a quick overview of his ideas and some things to watch for as we read. Wouldn't that be the best way to spend this evening?
HENRY: Why do you think it would be the best thing? Louise?
LOUISE: Lou, please. I was just nodding agreement with Maria. That sounds like a good idea.
HENRY: It may be, but I'm asking you why you think it is.
LOUISE: I gather that you don't think it's a good idea.
HENRY: I haven't said that. All I've indicated is an interest in why you think it's a good idea.
CRAIG: It is a good idea. It could save us hours and weeks of muddling around over difficult bits. We would know how to interpret Whitehead.
HENRY: Do you mean that you yourself would know how to interpret Whitehead, or that you would merely know how I would interpret Whitehead?
MARIA: What?
ANNE: He's asking if you want to play Follow My Leader.
FRANK: He's implying that some of you just want to be told what to think by teacher, because that is what you have all experienced as education, and

probably what most of us usually encourage our own students to do. Right, Henry?

HENRY: It could well be, but it might be somewhat different for each of us. What I am getting at, that is similar for all of us, is that we have here a question about "learning" in general and about our learning around Whitehead's ideas in particular. We are exploring what would be the best way for us to learn about Whitehead's ideas, are we not? If we just assume it is obvious, and the answer is that I should give a little lecture, why are we studying Whitehead? After all, most of the talks reproduced in the book were given to teachers, and put together in the way they are because Whitehead considered some of the most common notions about learning to be highly questionable, if not downright false. My impression is that one of his strongest themes is that "learning"—or rather, the best kind of learning to encourage, is an extremely difficult matter to clarify. And a great many teachers who think this is all too obvious are in fact muddled and encouraging the worst sort of learning, quite unwittingly.

LOUISE: I must say I can't see what's so difficult about the idea of learning. Is there a real difficulty or are we just splitting hairs?

HENRY: Well, if you don't see a difficulty, and I gave a little talk on Whitehead's theory of education, assuming there is a difficulty, you certainly would think I was splitting hairs, wouldn't you? And then you might go away and say about me what so many people say about philosophers—that I just spin out convoluted webs of words until I have convinced everyone there is a problem where really there wasn't one at all! (*Everyone laughs, except Louise, who is looking puzzled and irritable.*)

HENRY: Does anyone see my point?

MARIA: I'm getting the feeling that you're playing some kind of a game with us, and I don't like that.

ANNE: Maria, I don't see it that way. Isn't the point that as educators we need to be learning as much as we can about learning itself, otherwise we can't do the best possible for our students? If we come here to learn more about education, we also come here to learn more about learning, which is an essential part of education. If we assume from the start that we already know all we need to know about how to learn about Whitehead's ideas—or anything else—our minds are going to be closed to any important new insights about learning.

DAVID: I see something else here, I think. What's being assumed is that we know how we do our best learning, so we don't look critically at our own process of learning. All we look at is other people's ideas of learning, mostly in regard to children. But I'm not at all sure that in a general way our best type of learning is any different from children's—I mean, the other way round. So by not examining how we do, or might, go about our own best learning, we don't get valuable insights we could use to benefit our students.

FRANK: I seriously doubt whether we or our students know much about learning or even really want to. Certainly not about the things that are learned in school, anyway.

MARIA: Oh, Frank! Don't be so pessimistic. But I think I understand now why we're making a fuss about this. In order to be sure we aren't making wrong assumptions about learning, we have to throw the assumptions we are making into a critical light, by pretending they are wrong and see if they really can stand up after all that.

HENRY: Yes, that's pretty close to what I had in mind. And I'm in agreement with what Anne and David said, too. But surely the only way to test this process we are in now is for us to say first, what we think "learning" could mean; second, what it should mean for education; and third, what we usually do mean when we encourage students to do it. Then we can open all this to criticism. If it turns out we're splitting hairs, we can drop it and move on. Philosophy is a kind of difficult play for me, but it certainly isn't the kind of silly verbal magician's game it is often accused of being. My life is too short to dribble away on that sort of petty verbal one-upmanship. All right then, what does our term "learning" mean to you?

FRANK: (*smugly*) My experience with learning is that it's an activity of finding out about someone's nice little theory, thinking it's true, committing oneself to it, and then finding it's no good—over and over again.

JERRY: That doesn't apply to music. Or for some other arts. In music the important learning is some sort of combination of fiddling around on an instrument until the fingers begin to get a feel for making the instrument sound out the silent music in the mind. I mean, the combination of learning about an instrument and learning about how sounds become harmonies, discords, melodies, and so on.

CRAIG: I'm not sure about music, but so far as school is concerned, learning is finding out what experts have established—in science, history, and so on, and then learning how to apply it to solve problems in some area. I don't see how we could expect a fourteen-year-old to "fiddle around" by himself until he discovered the causes of the American War of Independence or the joint wave and particle characteristics of light.

HENRY: (*He thumbs quickly through his copy of* The Aims.) Hang on a moment. . . . Whitehead says something very similar. . . . Here it is:

> After all the child is the heir to long ages of civilization, and it is absurd to let him wander in the intellectual maze of men in the Glacial Epoch. Accordingly, a certain pointing out of important facts, and of simplify-

ing ideas, and of usual names, really strengthens the natural impetus of
the pupil.

GLENDA: Oh! I think that's wonderful! I'd never quite thought of teaching, I
mean the point of teaching, in that way. It makes so much sense.

CRAIG: I like it too. Where is it?

HENRY: Chapter Three, page 33, in this Free Press 1967 edition. (*Craig
scribbles quickly on a note pad.*)

LOUISE: I'm not sure how much I like it. It sounds pretty, but my kids are
right now getting what Whitehead suggests there, and their "natural impetus"
isn't strengthened—they're getting swamped, frustrated, and bored.

HENRY: Well, I have something for you here, Lou. On the previous page, he
says:

> This overhaste to impart mere knowledge defeats itself. The human mind
> rejects knowledge imparted in this way. The craving for expansion, for
> activity, inherent in youth is disgusted by a dry imposition of disciplined
> knowledge.

FRANK: When I was at school, and university, learning was mostly just
that—a disgustingly dry burden of stuff to memorize. If I asked what it was all
about, or why we had to memorize it, I got sat on for being disruptive,
cheeky, impertinent—and believe me, some of my teachers were big and
heavy!

MARIA: Thus speaketh Flat Frank. (*Frank scowls at the laughter, then lies
flat out on the rug as if run over by a steam roller.*)

LOUISE: Well, I think Frank has a good point. My schooling was often like
that, but I didn't think of questioning it, and didn't, until our kids started getting upset with it in grades one and two. Then I remembered I had the same
experience—though I didn't think to complain. I put my energy into learning
how to play the game so that I could get through and out without being flat-
tened and get on with what I really liked doing.

CRAIG: Before we go any further with these sad little stories, aren't we forgetting the reality is that a lot of really necessary learning is unavoidably a
plodding, difficult process, and needs self-discipline? Surely that's an important lesson to learn about life, isn't it, even if it hurts?

HENRY: A lot of important learning does have to go through plodding, difficult phases, yes—that's partly what Whitehead refers to as the stage of precision. But we should distinguish between unavoidable difficulty—the difficulty
inherent in the task itself, and the difficulty of learning when it's being made
artificially difficult for us.

ANNE: (*She has recently separated from her husband.*) You bet there's a difference! Learning is often painful, and you can learn from the pain. But the pain
of the learning itself is enough, without people adding to the difficulty with

their ignorance or anger . . . or just blind, stupid repetition of the destructive relationship patterns they were conditioned to. (*Silence drops over the room at the intensity and anger of Anne's pronouncement.*)

DAVID: (*diplomatic*) I noted something down earlier that I want to question. Henry, you said something about our wanting to learn about Whitehead's ideas on education, and Maria I think more or less went along with that assumption. But in a way that isn't what I want to do. This is what Frank was complaining about—continually learning merely what others have said. When I was writing in my journal I realized that I wasn't so much wanting to learn what Whitehead has to say as using him to trigger my own learning.

MARIA: You think you know better than Whitehead?

DAVID: No. You don't understand. I mean that I might come to agree with Whitehead, but only after I have seen the point for myself—but then it's not me having Whitehead's idea, but me having my own idea. It's no longer just me repeating what Whitehead has seen. It's what I haven't seen before, but do see now.

GLENDA: Yes, yes. I agree with that. Good point.

FRANK: And what if both you and Whitehead are wrong and don't realize it? How much does having seen it for yourself count then? This reminds me of some of the nonsense going on in "free schools"—everyone's utterly fanatical about kids discovering for themselves, but when you look at what they are discovering, much of it is confused and trivial. And often the teachers say nothing, even though they know it's wrong. The whole thing is absurd.

DAVID: Slow down, will you, Frank. You can't just wipe out the value of seeing for yourself like that, even if some free-schooling types get it a bit distorted. After all, if you're just repeating someone else's words, even if they do understand and are right, you yourself haven't learned it—the fact, I mean. All you've learned is that someone said it, and perhaps you have even believed it. But you haven't learned in the sense of understanding something about the topic, the issue itself. I know what Whitehead means when he talks of the problem of the dry imposition of adult knowledge turning students off, and I know he's right, because I've watched it happen in my own class at school. What I didn't see before thinking about his words was that this is a problem that we might be able to find a way past.

FRANK: Look. . . .

ANNE: So what you are saying, David, is that Whitehead suggested something, drew your attention to it in a new way, and then you saw or discovered something for yourself, realized it was true, and could justify its truth on the grounds of your own experience as a teacher. Whitehead was the trigger, but you did your own understanding, and that is what counts for you as the best kind of learning?

DAVID: You've got it. That's it exactly.

ANNE: All right, but I take Frank's point about the idiot fringe of the free school movement. There's no need to see the issue as black or white—either the students memorize and believe what the teacher says, or they discover everything for themselves. Surely a teacher can say and do things in such a way and at just the right time, so that the child discovers something for herself as a result.

FRANK: Sounds good in theory, but in practice . . . .

MARIA: Wait a minute. Don't just sit on this one as impractical, Frank, even if it is often difficult in practice. I was going to say that I have seen this "discover for yourself" idea taken to absurd limits, where any guidance from the teacher is excluded. I was once a teacher for a short while in an early childhood education center where the director had a huge poster in the hall which said something like: "You do your thing, and I'll do mine, and perhaps somewhere we shall meet."

FRANK: Oh no! What mush!

MARIA: Wait, I haven't finished. The next thing I remember is coming across the playground and seeing two little boys on the ground, one absolutely creaming the other—God, it was ugly—and this director just standing watching. I rushed in to stop them, and he stopped me, saying that they had to discover for themselves by experience that violence is not the way. I argued with him futilely, and then resigned. His attitude looks to me like dangerous foolishness, not respect for personal discovery in learning.

CRAIG: "You do your thing, and I'll do mine, and perhaps somewhere we shall meet?" Sounds to me like Newtonian atoms cruising around in space with only their own direction in mind, and occasionally smashing into one another! Great principle for a good life, that.

LOUISE: Yes, but don't go overboard. It also points to the fact that people are often meddling and interfering in others' lives and don't know what the heck they are doing. It also applies to people never being themselves and always living the way someone else wants them to, even if it kills them.

HENRY: And in a special sense it probably does. I think that's what Whitehead means when he talks about the problem of "soul murder" in schools—in Chapter Four.

DAVID: But I thought that there he was just talking dramatically about taking the enjoyment out of learning.

HENRY: He was, but he may be referring to a special kind of enjoyment, and perhaps continually taking that out of learning eventually causes an irreversible injury to the spirit of a human being.

GLENDA: (*upset*) What? What do you mean?

HENRY: Nothing that we can't discuss after we have taken a break to enjoy that enticing lemon meringue pie Louise has surreptitiously placed on the table behind you.

All heads turn, and difficult ideas are pushed aside as everyone begins to get up and head for the table, stretching legs and praising Louise for the sheer appearance of the enormous pie. David's attempt to tell them that he made it is drowned in a babble of conversation, while Lou smiles to herself, doing nothing to correct their assumption about the cook's identity. Slowly everyone finds their way back to where they were sitting and conversations die down. Henry Freedman is already sitting down, reading something in his copy of *The Aims*. An expectant silence settles over the room and is broken by Craig.

CRAIG: Look, it's not that I haven't enjoyed the discussion so far, but I can't see any definite way in which it can tell me what to do, or do differently, as a teacher in a classroom.
HENRY: (*He looks up and puts the book down.*) First Maria thinks that because I'm a professor who studies Whitehead I should tell her how to understand Whitehead. Now you, perhaps for the reason that I teach in an education faculty, seem to want me to tell you what to do in the classroom. I wonder why as a "teacher" it is assumed that I should be telling people what to think and what to do? Or was that not what you had in mind, Craig?
CRAIG: Well, I have to admit that I was hoping you might say something about what difference it makes to my classroom practice if I take Whitehead seriously. I don't think I was assuming that is your job just because you're a teacher in the area of education.
HENRY: All right, but the practical concern is bothering you?
CRAIG: Yes.
HENRY: I find that most student teachers, not to mention experienced teachers, are terribly impatient to get clear about practical details.
CRAIG: But the job of a teacher is nine tenths practical details. I don't see what is wrong with my impatience over that.
HENRY: But you, and the other teachers here, are already immersed in the practice of teaching—and I gather that your practicum supervisor thinks you are a capable practitioner.
DAVID: As one teacher here, Craig, I don't think of myself as being here primarily to find out what to do in the classroom, as if there were some all-embracing magical formula of techniques which will ensure the proper results under any circumstances. Of course, if what I do in school didn't change in some significant way as a result of the discussions I certainly would wonder if we were wasting our time.

GLENDA: I'm not even thinking about my classroom practice. I just love hearing all these ideas.

JERRY: So do I.

FRANK: Oh I just love everything about everything! (*Glenda begins to flash anger, but her attention is diverted by Craig.*)

CRAIG: Maybe, but I need to see some practical relevance to all this, and I don't see what's wrong with that.

HENRY: In itself, Craig, neither do I. I see it as a thoroughly necessary concern. My question, though, is whether you are putting the cart before the horse at the moment.

ANNE: I think he is. Surely we're here because we sense that there's a lot more to genuine educational practice than we can presently see or do. So we're here to find out something new in terms of ideas, and if we can, only then do we go into the question of what they imply for practice.

HENRY: Look at it this way. Craig, if you want to travel, what are you going to be thinking about?

CRAIG: Where I want to go and how I am going to get there.

HENRY: Yes. Which will you sort out first?

CRAIG: That depends. If I like sailing, I want to sail just about anywhere as long as I sail. So I'll be thinking of how to go wherever I end up going. But if it's important that I get somewhere specific, like Paris, where I want to go is my first concern. When that's settled, then I will think about how to get there. But why are we talking about this?

HENRY: I think you'll see in a few seconds. So you would not do something as silly as deciding, for example, that you would like to walk, before deciding on your destination—which if it is Paris would require some sea travel?

CRAIG: Obviously not, but .. . . .

HENRY: But isn't the situation for an educator somewhat similar? I mean, being quite sure where you have to go before deciding how to get there?

CRAIG: Yes, I suppose it is. Only if I know I'm going to teach math does it make sense to get hold of some math texts.

HENRY: Then you're quite sure that learning math is best accomplished by using math textbooks, and you're also quite sure that any kind of math learning will successfully convey the student to the destination of "being educated" or "having become educated"?

CRAIG: I'm confused now.

HENRY: In other words, are you so sure you know what your destination of "learning math" or of "becoming more educated through learning math" means? To the point where no question remains, and it then makes sense to focus entirely on how to get there—the practice?

CRAIG: Oh, I see. No. If "learning math" means just memorizing a few formulae and the standard ways to use them, I would know how to do that. But I wouldn't want to, because I don't think that is a good meaning for "learning math."

HENRY: So what do you think "learning math" ought to mean if it's supposed to be part of this aim to "educate"?

CRAIG: It should mean things like understanding why we have those formulae, why it's necessary to know them, how they could be used in situations the student has never met before . . . .

FRANK: Wait a minute. That wasn't what mathematics meant, or what its importance was, to Pythagoras, or Descartes, or Pascal, or Riemann, or Einstein, or Gödel, and these are the great mathematicians. If you followed Pythagoras, you would probably be getting Jerry into your class with one of his cellos so that the kids could study the relationship of the tone of the sound to the length of the string vibrating . . . .

JERRY: The pitch of the sound, not the tone.

FRANK: Well, whatever.

CRAIG: I can't believe you're serious, Frank. Twentieth-century students need to learn the math they are going to have to understand in offices, in engineering, in calculating their income tax . . . .

HENRY: So the educational aim in learning math in schools is part of the aim at learning to function in employment and other social contexts where specialist knowledge and skills are required? Learning to do all that is what "education" in schools should mean, is it?

CRAIG: Look, I don't know if I could say what "education" ought to mean, but I know what it currently means in schools. It means precisely what you said, Henry, and our students would hardly thank us if it didn't. Remember that outcry and lawsuit in New York over a boy who graduated from high school but could hardly read?

HENRY: I never implied that the schools have no responsibility for such learning. I'm quite sure they do. But is that the whole of the meaning of "education," or even the most important part of it, once we understand what the most significant meaning of "education" is?

LOUISE: Well, what on earth is the most significant meaning?

FRANK: And how could we be sure if that meaning is the most significant?

HENRY: If we had a statement about what that meaning is, then we could work out ways of checking whether it is correct, and why. Until we have some statements as to what might be the best meaning for "education," isn't discussion of how to validate a meaning premature? Let me get something clear. Does everyone here agree that the point of school teaching is to educate, or not?

MARIA: I don't know what you mean, or what should be meant by "education" any more. I just know that it is important for children in school to learn to read, write, communicate well in speech, be able to do some math, and things like that. Isn't that educating? How could educating be more significant than that? I'm lost.

GLENDA: No, I think this is good. I've done lots of those things in school, and done them well enough to be a schoolteacher myself, and to be able to get along in society pretty well, but right now I'm not at all sure I could describe myself as "educated." I have a feeling there is something more than all this needed for education. It's exciting, and I feel it, but I couldn't say what it is.

HENRY: Is there anyone here who could say with complete assurance, and give adequate reasons for that assurance, that he or she as parent or teacher is definitely educating the children in his or her care? (*silence*) No one! I take it, then, that if we really are in doubt as to whether we know what "education" should mean, and therefore in doubt as to what anyone would need to do in order to educate, none of us can be sure that we are educating at all! Right?

FRANK: Right. But does it matter?

HENRY: Does it matter to you, Louise, so far as your children are concerned?

LOUISE: You bet it does. Although I couldn't say what the best meaning for "educate" would be, like Glenda I have a strong feeling that it would refer to something very humanly important. I don't want my children fouled up because there happens to be a heck of a muddle over that, especially if no one is bothering to try to sort the muddle out.

HENRY: What is the title of Whitehead's book on education?

MARIA: *The Aims of Education and Other Essays.*

HENRY: Precisely.

CRAIG: Precisely what? What's the point?

HENRY: Whitehead is writing in an effort to get some clarity on just this very point.

CRAIG: What point?

ANNE: The point that there is considerable doubt and confusion over the proper meaning of "educate," leading to all sorts of wrong practices in schools?

HENRY: Yes, that's it, Anne. When we talk about something like "educate," we have certain purposes, achievements, aims, in mind. So when we ask what the most significant meaning of "education" would be, we are asking what we ought to aim for if we want to genuinely educate. And there is a great deal of confusion over this. That's surely why Whitehead, in his talks with teachers in this book, wants to go into the matter of the proper aims of education in great depth. Is that a good point to stop for this evening? I'm getting tired, and most of you look as though you're wilting fast.

DAVID: Yes, I'd say that's more than enough to think about until next time. Is everyone able to meet at the same time in two weeks?

GLENDA: I'd rather meet before that. What about next Sunday? (*A general chorus of agreement ensues.*)

DAVID: Well fine. I'll go along with that. What about some kind of preparation for the next session? Just a quick first read of Chapters One to Seven?

HENRY: Yes, though the first chapter contains so much that I would suggest a careful reading of it and some questions jotted down. The only other thing I would like to say before we all head off is that I'd be glad to have you all at my place next week. David and Lou have looked after us well this evening, and I think it would be good to spread the load.

Everyone starts getting up to go, writing down Henry's address, putting on coats and saying good-byes. Some look wistfully at the remains of the pie.

# Four

# SECOND DIALOGUE: THE DYING MIND

**Sunday, 12 November**

Henry Freedman and Maria are sitting by the wall-length windows of Henry's small, one-story home on a piece of land on the edge of town. The windows overlook a rough meadow, which ends a hundred yards from the bank of a stream. They are sipping wine, saying nothing, as the contemplative notes of Keith Jarrett's jazz piano expand and fill the room in the waning light, leaving no space for words. Maria's offer to come over and help Henry with the dinner had been gratefully accepted; he does not enjoy serious cooking by himself. The growing sound of a car engine mingles with the piano, and they both look up to see Jerry's small sports car churning down the drive at twice the normal speed for a residential driveway.

Soon other cars follow, and the kitchen and living room are buzzing with conversation. A sense of more definite purpose is in the air this week. Many copies of *The Aims* are lying around the room, together with scribbled and typed notes and a smattering of other books. Henry's roving academic eye subconsciously takes in the red cover of Whitehead's *Modes of Thought*, and two copies of the familiar purple of *Science and the Modern World*.

An hour later, around six-thirty, everyone is seated, with coffee or a glass of wine, and the buzz of conversation slowly dies in anticipation of serious dialogue. Henry begins.

HENRY: That's surprising. Everyone is here.
GLENDA: Why surprising, Henry?
HENRY: Once sampled, the convólutions of philosophical inquiry don't always sit well with many people.
MARIA: You mean we were doing philosophy last week? I didn't even realize that. Why was it philosophical?
HENRY: Does anyone here think he or she grasps what being philosophical is, so as to be able to put it in a sentence or two?
ANNE: There's some difference of opinion amongst philosophers themselves over what they're supposed to be doing. I think of it this way: when someone starts getting philosophical . . . .
FRANK: They start getting hopelessly tangled up in words.
MARIA: Be quiet, Frank. In any case, I don't think we got hopelessly tangled up last week.
LOUISE: Maybe it's just that you're afraid of being without hope, Frank.
FRANK: Good heavens! Can I come to you for therapy?
HENRY: Frank, come out of your sniper's tree and let Anne finish.

ANNE: Oh, I thought that was getting interesting. Well, I was going to say, before I was so cynically interrupted, that when people start getting "philosophical," they start asking questions. Not just any old questions, but questions about assumptions that everyone else regards as so obviously true they wouldn't even think consciously of them, let alone frame a question about them. I mean, it's just the same as when most of the time we walk around on the floor but never notice the floor itself. In a philosophical moment we suddenly notice something about the floor itself and begin examining it. Perhaps we see a split board or a woodworm hole and wonder if the floor is safe after all.

DAVID: I like that, Anne. It fits what we were doing last week and what Whitehead seems to be doing in his education book. Craig, for example, wanted to know what to do, assuming the solidity of the floor, but Henry asked if he was sure of the floor itself . . . .

JERRY: The "floor" here being assumptions about what the proper aims of education are?

HENRY: Or the chief aim of education, when wisely understood?

JERRY: Yes, I would say so.

DAVID: Yes, that's what I mean: the overall aims are more the ground ideas on which everything is built.

MARIA: But after reading Whitehead I can't say he sounded like the one or two philosophy books I've read—I mean, I don't find him easy. But it still reads like . . . like, well, like real English. (*Her last word is drowned in laughing from the rest of the group, she starts in surprise, and then joins in.*)

HENRY: As a matter of fact you're right, Maria. He doesn't sound quite like a philosopher speaking to other philosophers, because after all he isn't. He's talking to teachers and other people in education, probably very few of whom could follow a formal philosophical presentation.

MARIA: But then is he doing philosophy?

HENRY: Yes, because although he's not doing it in the technical way of modern philosophy, he's still doing what Anne and David were describing— examining the ground of ideas on which the whole enterprise stands. But he's expressing what he sees in a more conversational way, so as to be intelligible to non-philosophers.

JERRY: I can't say I always find him intelligible. (*A chorus of murmured agreement ensues.*)

HENRY: No. But that's the difficulty. Philosophers have to look at apparently ordinary things in a most unordinary way, if they are to see the unordinary aspects of them. It's the same for a botanist talking about backyard plants. Then to communicate, you have the task of expressing these unusual thoughts in a language designed mainly for use in expressing quite ordinary things. This is the challenge Whitehead is facing in his writing. If you don't see that, you may dismiss much of what he says as obscure when a little persistence would bring his meaning through.

JERRY: Yes, I can see you could, though that wasn't the effect on me. In the bits I couldn't understand I still had a strong sense of him saying something really interesting, but on some level of awareness I haven't properly reached.

GLENDA: Well, I just loved—I mean, I found his discussion quite fascinating. Oh, stop grinning so smugly, Frank!

HENRY: All right, the capacity to be open enough to be inspired is a precious thing, and we don't have to be carried away by it into a naive lack of critical awareness.

FRANK: Can we get on to discussing Chapter One? I thought that was our business tonight?

HENRY: Yes, and it is. But in an important sense we already have, since to discuss a piece of writing fruitfully, we have to be sure what kind of writing it is. If we read science fiction as a factual account of life on other planets we would be in a tremendous muddle. So we need to be clear that Whitehead is seeing his topic as a philosopher, roughly what that implies, and that he is experiencing the difficulty of conveying philosophic questions and insights in ordinary language. It's like trying to follow verbal directions in a strange city. You know the words well enough, but often you wish you had a map as well.

There is another analogy I sometimes use in conveying the sense of what philosophy is. I'll quickly tell you before we move on. The philosopher—and he or she doesn't have to be an academic—is like an unusual person at a cinema who doesn't want to just follow the movie, but instead wants the projectionist to show the film one frame at a time so that she can examine precisely how the impression of a living scene could arise.

Philosophers try to slow life to a stop to see what ultimately makes it tick, or what's wrong with our conception of it, just as we stop a car and turn off the engine before putting our hands in the works. Of course, if all you want to do is rush off somewhere, especially if you think there is nothing wrong with the car, this approach would be very annoying. Sometimes in educational meetings you periodically hear someone say in exasperation, "Oh, don't start getting philosophical! We have to do something!" People in education, and almost any other walk of life, get impatient when their continuity of action is threatened with a major overhaul of the basic ideas on which the whole operation runs. Oops! That's two analogies, I know, but I honestly didn't realize the car was coming. All right, let's consider the first chapter.

MARIA: Am I going to be jumped on if I ask you for a quick summation?

HENRY: No, again just politely and purposefully refused.

MARIA: I really don't understand this refusal of yours.

HENRY: And you might not understand why I also won't explain my refusal. But if you get an idea as to why I have refused, I'd like to know—and I promise to answer then.

MARIA: Okay, Mr. Mystery Man. (*laughter*)

HENRY: I'm sure that if I say I'm not mystery-mongering you won't believe me. But let's get on, shall we? Where do you want to start?

CRAIG: I know where I want to start. At the beginning of the chapter I thought it was clear that inert ideas are the overall theme. But as I went on I couldn't see how everything tied in with this, and now I don't know how all the bits hang together. Why is he also talking about culture, the nature of the mind, the independence of the curriculum of each school, "style"—whatever that is. . . . And how on earth does the last bit about education being religious fit with anything? I was fighting off the temptation to accuse him of being thoroughly disorganized and perhaps self-indulgent in just scattering his personal convictions around like confetti.

HENRY: If we are to keep our critical wits we can't dismiss that possibility, but let's at least start by being generous and assuming hypothetically that he knows exactly what he's talking about, and that it's all unified. Then, if it is, we at least have a chance of finding out how. To start with, since you mention it, what about these inert ideas? What would you say inert ideas are?

GLENDA: I doubt whether we could improve on what Whitehead says... here, on the first page of Chapter One: "inert ideas . . . are merely received into the mind without being . . . ."

HENRY: Just a minute, Glenda. For a start I think you're forgetting that we've all read that passage, and in addition, I asked what you would say, not what Whitehead says. We know what Whitehead says.

GLENDA: What's wrong with using Whitehead's words, if I doubt that they can be improved upon?

HENRY: A great deal, perhaps. After all, this is not a discussion in the area of literary appreciation.

GLENDA: I don't see what you're getting at.

DAVID: I think I do, and I found this out in a new way while I was writing in my journal. I would look at what sounded like a fine passage of Whitehead's, sense that something really important to me was being said, but it was only after I messed around up one blind alley and down another, and got it into my own words eventually, to my own satisfaction, that I felt I truly understood what he meant. Then I could begin to be guided in my own life by that idea. My words certainly are not as eloquent, but they carry all the weight of whatever understanding I have, not Whitehead's. His carry the weight of his understanding, not mine.

HENRY: Can you put that insight into a general principle, David? (*pause*) No? Well, can anyone?

ANNE: I'll have a go at it. Let's see . . . only if we can express an idea adequately in our own words, can we be sure that the words used express a genuine personal understanding. How's that?

HENRY: It certainly captures what was on my mind. Would the principle apply to reading poetry? You look uncertain; so am I. So we are not yet sure just how far the principle can be generalized, but so far as it does go, I think it expresses an important truth. Glenda, you look quite unconvinced. Try this: can you tell me how you would recognize if one of your students had an "inert" idea?

GLENDA: The student wouldn't seem interested or excited by the idea.

HENRY: Probably not, though it's a moot point whether any and every kind of interest is absent if an idea is inert. But for the most part, I agree with you. Why do you think that this student might seem uninterested, so that for him the idea is inert?

GLENDA: Well, he might find interest in a number of things, all the way from feeling loved and secure in his family to skateboarding with his friends, but the idea doesn't connect with any of this. Whatever the idea is supposed to say to him, or anyone else, he doesn't care about it.

HENRY: But he might still pass an exam on it.

GLENDA: Yes, of course; I remember doing lots of that myself. But he would have forgotten all about it within a month. It would be useless to him as an adult.

HENRY: Do you mean he would not be able to use it—apart from passing the exam, and perhaps impressing his parents by spouting it at them?

GLENDA: Yes, it would be useless to him because he wouldn't be able to use it.

HENRY: If you are going to escape a charge of tautology, you'd better tell us just why he wouldn't be able to use it.

GLENDA: Because he doesn't care about it.

HENRY: Suppose he does come to care about it much later. Let's suppose the idea is "love." He had to read about it in some of Shakespeare's sonnets in school, but now he is in an intense relationship with a woman. He finds that all he can do is boss her around, and that puts her off, which is exactly what he doesn't want. He realizes he's no good at being loving, and yet he passed his exams on this idea.

GLENDA: Oh, I think I see. He can't use the idea because he didn't really understand it. No, wait, I can say it better than that. He only understood how to talk about the idea, but never really understood the reality that the idea and all the talk were supposed to be about. Heavens! What am I saying? Is that all nonsense?

LOUISE: If Henry thinks it is, I'm on your side against him. I mean, that sounds really clear and right to me, and I will think Henry is wrong if he says "nay" to it.

HENRY: Hey, take it easy, ladies. I'm on your side, honest! Seriously, I quite agree that that popped out with a wonderful clarity, Glenda. And, note, they're your words, not Whitehead's.

CRAIG: I think our imaginary student did understand something about the idea of love. It couldn't be just a sheer memorization of Shakespeare's and the teacher's words, because the exam would require the words to be put in a different combination, or in answer to a question he hadn't seen before.

LOUISE: Yes, I agree with that, but I think the understanding is far too shallow, far too attached to someone else's speech to be of much use when needed in day-to-day living. So this man thinks he is loving the woman, but really he mostly wants to possess her—and probably use her sexually—and this comes out as being controlling, or bossing her about. He thinks he loves, but expresses a sort of abuse and can't understand how there could be such a contradiction. But if you said to him, in some comfortable little exam, "Is abuse love?" he would answer "No," and get ten out of ten. (*Frank has begun wagging his finger at David, with an affected knowing look, and the group dissolves in laughter.*)

HENRY: This is all right, I'm sure, so far as the meaning of the inertness of an idea is concerned. I think you're claiming, in effect, that in a context like school it's easy to confuse the understanding of an idea and what it refers to with what is mostly just an understanding of what people, like teachers, or writers, say about the idea and the area of life it refers to. Is that it? (*A murmur of general agreement follows.*)

So, even if you can play at passing exams—because most exams don't challenge real understanding—in actual life what could be the point of having ideas if they remain inert?

FRANK: Oh, I don't know, they are rather useful for impressing people at cocktail parties with the illusion that you know a lot about many things when really you know almost nothing.

ANNE: Quite so, Frank, but life is not all cocktail parties. It's also war, unemployment, political intrigue, bringing up difficult children, children having to cope with slightly insane parents, separation and divorce after getting secure in the feeling that people love you and want to spend the rest of their life with you, and so on. This is a big chunk of the rest of daily life and nowhere here are cute words going to impress anyone, or show any light at the end of the tunnel. (*The force of passion and unassailable truth coming from Anne silences everyone into a new thoughtfulness.*)

HENRY: What's the connection between not caring much about the idea, and only understanding it shallowly—so that it can't help one to understand phases of one's life even where it is the appropriate idea? (*silence*)

Try this then. Remember that Glenda, and then Anne, were tremendously intense and caring about the ideas they were exploring? And what happened? Out came something with depth, clarity, importance, truth. Now these things—truth, clarity, depth, importance, and the like, what aspect of a person do they require to be very active?

FRANK: The intelligence, I suppose.

HENRY: Exactly. Now my question is: is there a significant connection between interest, caring, and intelligence?

JERRY: Yes, there is, though I hadn't seen it quite like this before. I would say that your intelligence can't be really effective unless what you are dealing with seems to have a great deal of importance. I mean, the importance must be personally felt, mustn't it?

FRANK: Must it? Why?

JERRY: Well, see how it works in music. When people really like a piece and are moved by it, they tend to learn it quickly and play it much better, with feeling—some special personal touch.

HENRY: With style—a style of their own?

JERRY: Yes.

CRAIG: Are you meaning the same "style" that Whitehead talks about towards the end of the chapter?

HENRY: Very likely, but let's go slowly here, or we might miss the fact that Whitehead keeps on coming back in one way or another to this crucial idea of education needing to be concerned with an intelligence that is active, and by the very nature of mind this has to begin with the individual's personal feeling for the significance of the subject-matter . . . .

CRAIG: That's it! It's right here between the lines in his discussion of "style." Look, on page 13 he says, "With style your power is increased, for your mind is not distracted with irrelevancies, and you are more likely to attain your object."

FRANK: It's on page 3 as well: "the first thing to do with an idea is . . . to prove its worth. . . . In our first contact with a set of propositions, we commence by appreciating their importance."

GLENDA: Well, what about this on page 2: "Let the main ideas . . . be few and important. . . . The child should make them his own, and should understand their application here and now in the circumstances of his actual life."

MARIA: Look at this then, on page 6: "Whatever interest attaches to your subject-matter must be evoked here and now." He is really heavy on the present, the here and now, isn't he?

DAVID: Or on page 11 he says: "The specialist side of education presents an easier problem than does the provision of a general culture. . . . But undoubtedly the chief reason is that the specialist study is normally a study of peculiar interest to the student." And listen to this: "He is studying it because, for some reason, he wants to know it. This makes all the difference."

HENRY: Did you see on the same page, at the bottom: "one of the ways of encouraging general mental activity is to foster a special devotion?"

DAVID: No, that passed me by, but I see that it fits.

CRAIG: Even on the last page of the chapter, in this passage on education being religious—which puzzles me—he hints at the importance of interest to the activation of intelligence when he highlights "reverence." After all, when reverence occurs, as in religion, a really special kind of interest is present, something like awe, respect, wonder—I don't know how to talk about it.

JERRY: I know what you're getting at, even though I don't know anything about religion. Because in music you can have reverence. Periodically I suddenly lose my familiarity with Bach, and I am struck dumb by the sheer wonder of it. That's like reverence, isn't it?

HENRY: Yes.

JERRY: And that reverence is a tremendous interest, a tremendous respect, and, yes, a sense of profound understanding, of intelligence recognizing with a rare kind of power something of enormous importance. Intelligence is there, understanding, even though you can't really put in words what you understand. I suppose that's why people often say that kind of appreciation is "just" a feeling.

MARIA: Can we take a break? I need to let some of this digest for a while!

HENRY: Well, why don't you show everyone what you helped to make for the good of their digestion—or their palates at least!

People get up, stretch, and saunter vaguely towards the kitchen, picking up glasses of almost untouched wine and cups of cold coffee they realize with surprise they had completely forgotten. Glenda has a sudden private idea about why Socrates didn't get drunk in the *Symposium* and smiles to herself. Henry suspects that everyone will have had enough for one night, even though he feels awake and alive. But ten minutes later the group is calling him out of a corner where he and Frank are sharing a joke.

DAVID: Come on, Henry, Frank, we're ready to carry on. (*Henry and Frank join the group and everyone settles down.*)

ANNE: During the break, what we've been discussing all seems to have fallen into place for me, and I'd like to say it while it's still in place. (*She pauses, staring intently at one wall.*)

FRANK: Go on, then.

ANNE: All right, this is how I see it. In education, we want to help children to understand things we consider important to them—and to all of us. And because these things are important, if they are, they're important enough to warrant being understood as deeply as possible. So, in the light of this, what Whitehead is claiming—and I agree—is that this really significant understanding can only be activated, because of the way we are by nature, if there is sufficient interest in what is being studied. And then the whole chapter falls together as all sorts of comments on this relation of interest and intelligence, how interest shows itself, ways in which it can be encouraged—and ways in which it can be, and is, killed. When it is killed, or never given birth to, the only type of learning possible is a caricature of learning—the clothes but not the living person underneath, so to speak. And in this caricature of learning the mind works with what Whitehead calls inert ideas.

LOUISE: That's nice, Anne. Yes, that pulls it together really well for me—in fact it adds a few useful bits I hadn't quite got before.

FRANK: It pulls it together rather too nicely for me. I'm getting very uncomfortable about the way I teach these days. I think I'm squarely in the inert ideas brigade. It's a depressing thought.

HENRY: Or, if you look at it another way, it could be an exciting thought. You might anticipate seeing some curious little changes coming about in your teaching next week—changes that you and your students will like.

FRANK: Well, we'll see.

HENRY: Yes, let's see . . . all of us, and discuss any interesting changes with each other. Because if no changes are detectable, the usefulness of what we are doing together is really called into question, isn't it?

JERRY: Maybe . . . but I'm not sure that my enjoyment of these sessions would be taken away if I didn't see any changes.

MARIA: If there were no changes at all, wouldn't that mean our discussions are really at the level of inert ideas?

HENRY: That question has occurred to me at times in the past, in other situations, and it's not an easy one. I mean, if there weren't any changes in practice, it would seem to indicate that any understanding we're getting here is pretty shallow. On the other hand, you all seem to be genuinely interested, even passionate at times, about the ideas that come up. Whitehead's sense of "inert" implies an utter lack of any passion around an idea.

If we are passionate but nothing noticeable is changing, that might indicate a disconnection of the ideas into an intellect separated from our actual living. The intellect is only one side of intelligence. So we would be enjoying the ideas in isolation just for their fascinating connections simply as ideas, and the accompanying images of ideal situations. After all, ideas do seem to have a special kind of beauty just in themselves, though some haven't experienced this. They can be enjoyed simply for their beauty—rather like colors combined into a delightful painting, and no obvious connection with life is needed. In itself I can't see anything wrong with this.

But when we are not reflecting, but rather in the midst of an action, life demands all kinds of understanding of itself at every point—or else! To get stuck in ideas as mere vehicles for tourist travel in outer mental space is then a real problem. I think that's the problem people hint at when they accuse university professors of living in "ivory towers." Often, when work seems to be especially pressured, I admit I wish fervently they were right!

FRANK: (*He breaks into a wicked smile.*) And they aren't?

HENRY: No, Frank, they are not! I'm just reading a novel set in Harvard by May Sarton, and if I can find it, I'm going to read you a few sentences. (*He rummages in a bag full of books and papers, pulls out a paperback and rapidly thumbs through it, stopping suddenly.*) Here it is: "In Small, the University was the world. The same splits broke it into pieces, the same tensions were working inside it, like fine fissures which might suddenly gape." Whatever we might like, Frank, we do take our world into the university with us—and often take too much of it. Then we turn the university into something it should not be, so far as educating is concerned. That's one good reason why Whitehead wrote the chapter, "Universities and Their Function." He thought that like schools they brought in too many things which worked against their best and most distinctive purpose. That chapter, written in 1928, first appeared in *Atlantic Monthly,* and perhaps it was an early start to the hot debate over the universities, in that journal and others, which Whitehead started up in the thirties.

ANNE: Who was the debate between?

HENRY: Oh, Robert Hutchins, Albert Levi.

ANNE: I'd like to read that. Do you have the references?

HENRY: Yes, write me a reminder and I'll look them up for you during the week, but I know that Whitehead sparked it off with his 1936 article in *Atlantic Monthly,* "Harvard: The Future." The Canadian scholar, A.H. Johnson, put it in his useful collection of Whitehead essays, called *Whitehead's American Essays in Social Philosophy.*

DAVID: I read a bit of that essay a while back . . . no, the one in the same book, called "Historical Changes," where he's talking about misconceptions of history as a curriculum subject—at least, that's what I think he was doing.

HENRY: What did he say?

DAVID: Well, I don't really know, because as soon as I came to the saying, "As we think, we live," my thoughts dived off on a tangent of their own and never came back to the essay.

MARIA: "As we think, we live?" I like that. Somehow it seems to capture what chapter one of *The Aims* is about. I mean, it's to do with the idea that unless we really think, really use our intelligence, instead of playing around with inert ideas, we don't really live.

DAVID: No, that's not what he means . . . .

HENRY: Hang on a moment, David. Let's see what Maria has got here.

MARIA: Well, he talks about women who have all this vitality because they aren't burdened by inert ideas. (*She is peering at page 2.*) And here he talks of subjects "not illumined with any spark of vitality."

GLENDA: And there's "deadly harm" on page 3, and . . . wait a moment . . . here it is: "the problem of keeping knowledge alive." That's on page 5.

DAVID: What about this one, then? This I really like—it's in the chapter on universities: "For successful education there must always be a certain freshness in the knowledge dealt with. . . . Knowledge does not keep any better than fish."

GLENDA: Where is that?

DAVID: Page 98.

JERRY: Does this have anything to do with the "soul-murder" you were talking about before, Henry?

HENRY: A lot, I'm sure. Those quotes are good ones, but let's not get lost in a quote-throwing spree. There's something we missed: Whitehead's emphasis not just on the educational uselessness of inert ideas, but the sheer harm of them. Look at page 1, at the bottom: "Education with inert ideas is not only useless: it is, above all things, harmful—*Corruptio optimi, pessima.*" Does anyone translate Latin well here?

LOUISE: It's been a long time, but what I've written over it in my copy is: "The corruption of the best is the worst of all." How's that?

HENRY: That's pretty well as I read it. Now that's a strong statement, isn't it? Presumably the best is what he calls "alive" knowledge or "culture"—you know, top of page 1—"activity of thought, and receptiveness to beauty and humane feeling." His argument, in effect, is that preoccupation with ideas that are held as inert ensures the certain death of that "best."

ANNE: I'd like to change his words in the quote which has the Latin phrase. I wish he wouldn't say "education with inert ideas," because his whole point is surely that if you are dealing with ideas which for you are inert, education is not happening, even though schooling is. What I get is that if you're preoccupied with ideas that are inert, you thereby immediately cancel the possibility of education—"wisely understood," as I remember you said, Henry.

HENRY: Yes, I agree with you. But we're so used to equating education with whatever goes on in schools or equally loosely, with any kind of institutional or other learning, that I suspect no one is very moved by the idea that even if schooling is going on, educating is not. So can you explain what this "education" essentially implies for you when you talk so gravely about its demise under the weight of inert ideas?

ANNE: Well, you said it yourself, Henry, just now when you emphasized not just "mind" but "activity of mind." (*Everyone looks quite lost.*) No? Let's see. . . . Look at page 6, at the top, no, the middle. Whitehead talks of

> one of the most fatal, erroneous, and dangerous conceptions ever introduced into the theory of education. The mind is never passive; it is a perpetual activity, delicate, receptive, responsive to stimuli. You cannot postpone its life until you have sharpened it.

HENRY: If the mind is "never passive," and if you get inert ideas by passive reception, then on this understanding of the term "mind," the mind is barely used at all when inert ideas predominate.

ANNE: Yes, but that's not quite what I'm getting at. I agree that where "mind" refers to intelligence, if inert ideas predominate then the mind is not active. Intelligence is an activity—the activity of discerning what is crucial and what is trivial, what is true and what is false. But what I'm after is another notion of Whitehead's that is flashing at me like a neon sign. Whitehead is suggesting—no, stating as a fact—that the mind is an "alive" process, it's "organic," not mechanical or an object like a container to hold things. Where is it that he discusses this?

DAVID: Chapter Three, I think. Around page 38 . . . yes, here it is, 38 and 39.

ANNE: Right. Okay, so the point is that the mind is alive, meaning that it is a living organism of some sort. So if it's not active it's wasting away.

CRAIG: What? How do you get that?

ANNE: Simple, Craig. Look at your legs . . . (*Someone calls out immediately, "Yes, let's see your legs, Craig," and the intense atmosphere breaks up with laughter as Craig rolls up one leg of his jeans and peers intently at his shin. Anne waits with an affected irritation while Craig rolls down his jeans again and things quiet down.*)

ANNE: Very funny. Now, can I say what I have to say, and then you can all act like complete idiots as much as you like?

FRANK: It's a deal, Anne.

ANNE: What I was trying to say to Craig was that his legs are organic. . . . (*Some quiet guffaws mingle with whispered remarks like, "They're really organic? No? No fertilizers or preservatives?" Anne labors on, ignoring them.*) And because they're organic they have to be active. If he sits down for ten years and doesn't use them at all, they will waste away. But if he walks and runs a lot, they get strong and develop.

LOUISE: He must be exercising then. I think his legs are very nicely developed.

ANNE: For goodness sake, Louise, can't even the women stand together here?

LOUISE: Depends how developed their legs are, honey.

HENRY: All right! All right! I think we should quiet down and let Anne finish now. I have a vested interest in what I think she's saying, and if you don't get it, you don't get Whitehead—period!

ANNE: All I'm saying is this: if the mind is organic, like all organic things it can only stay alive, replenish itself, grow, by the special activity appropriate to what it is. When schooling unwittingly involves students with inert ideas, their minds are inert. Therefore, their minds are slowly dying. So whatever they think they are doing, the teachers are systematically killing the students' minds. Heavens, isn't that why Whitehead is so outraged at the end of the chapter? Page 14. Listen to it.

> When one considers in its length and breadth the importance of this question of the education of the nation's young, the broken lives, the defeated hopes, the national failures, which result from the frivolous inertia with which it is treated, it is difficult to restrain within oneself a savage rage.

That's a very angry man, isn't it? Angry because any intelligent person would be angry who could see that a dying mind is a dying human being. Or, put it another way: if you can't get angry at the thought, the sight, of one-time human beings reduced to cunning vegetables at best, then you've already become one yourself! (*The few remaining smiles in the group disappear as Anne glares around for recognition of the point.*)

JERRY: Take it easy, Anne.

ANNE: I will not take it easy. I can't possibly laugh with you when that is on my mind, and I thank God I'm not yet dead enough to be able to treat an issue like that with cold detachment, our precious little caricature of "objectivity!"

HENRY: (*thoughtfully*) Yes, indeed, that would be a long way from "sensitivity to . . . humane feeling." However, there is also warm detachment, and that is important, wouldn't you say?

LOUISE: Yes, but that may have to come after feelings have been vented.

HENRY: Agreed, so long as it does come. But I'm not at all negating your point, especially since I don't believe the popular myth that anger always cancels reasonableness. Anger that is not egocentric often seems a necessary part of grasping the full weight of a terrible truth. I see Whitehead's anger there as being just that. (*A long, charged silence settles on the room.*)

GLENDA: (*She is thinking out loud.*) A "warm detachment"—that's a beautiful idea.

FRANK: Maybe—whatever it's supposed to mean, but I for one am tired, and it's late. Shall we call a halt? (*The group gives a chorus of agreement.*)

DAVID: And shall we settle something about our next meeting?

GLENDA: I would like everyone to come to my apartment next time. Here is the address. (*She writes on a scrap of paper and passes it round.*)

DAVID: Fine. At Glenda's. Any ideas about what to focus on next time?

CRAIG: I don't want to move on just yet. There are too many details in that first chapter I'd like to get straight.

DAVID: I'm for going into the second and third chapters, on romance, precision and generalization.

HENRY: How about this, then? We all run through chapter one again, but also prepare Chapters Two and Three, and then we can go just as far as we want to with all that.

JERRY: Then can we meet in two weeks? I've got a lot on, and I don't want to come with my mind full of other things and unprepared. (*After some indecision everyone eventually agrees, and a general exodus begins. Maria's voice cuts through the noise.*)

MARIA: Listen a moment. Henry is having difficulty with high tech. He doesn't have a dishwasher. Can anyone stay awhile and help clear up?

FRANK: Sure, I can. No problem.

ANNE: Me too.

MARIA: Thanks, we don't need more than two. Goodnight, everyone.

HENRY: Oh Jerry . . . there's no prize for first one out of the driveway.

JERRY: What? Oh! That's no way to speak to a plodding weekend driver like me.

Jerry is pushed out the door by Glenda, who is going with him and eager to get some sleep before a heavy week. The others stroll out after them, followed by the faint sound of running taps and the clink of dropped cutlery.

# Five

# THIRD DIALOGUE: MUCH ADO ABOUT AIMS

### Sunday, 26 November

Glenda's apartment is small, and everyone is rather cramped. There are no signs of complaint though, perhaps because they are beginning to feel a sense of communality creeping into their time together. During the week, when David remarked to Louise that dissent is a sign that people have begun to become comfortable with one another, Louise had replied, "I think that's similar to something A.S. Neill once said to the effect that there is perfect acceptance when we can walk past each other without any ritual acknowledgment of the other being necessary." David didn't understand the similarity, but Louise was already on her way up to see if the children were cleaning their teeth.

David's renewed reflection on this puzzle is interrupted by an offer of more coffee by Jerry, after a fine curry he and Glenda devised together. Maria chides the group for wasting away the evening in food and gossip. A few retorts fly in her direction, but she has touched an answering chord in them, for they are already moving into a rough circle for discussion.

DAVID: Purely out of self-interest I'm going to steal the start of the show with a problem for Whitehead . . . .
LOUISE: Whatever happened to democracy? We should decide by vote.
FRANK: Sentimental nonsense! Let this Nietzschean Overman guide the herd. Come on, David, claim your mountain top and play Goliath! We will believe anything you say.
DAVID: Thanks, Frank. Alas, my joy at your support is tinged by an unpleasant whiff of your insincerity.
HENRY: I vote that since David initiated the discussion meetings we indulge him for this once, presumptuous or not. (*Interrupting remarks come from various people: "Goliath is about to meet his stone." "As one of the herd, I'm worried about his knowledge of buffalo jumps."*) What's on your mind, David?
DAVID: All right, hear ye. Recently I read some stuff by Michael Oakeshott which Anne loaned me, and I was just getting nicely carried along when . . . .
CRAIG: What stuff?
DAVID: Oh. (*He looks at the sheets in his hand.*) An essay called "Education: The Engagement and its Frustration," in a collection called *Education and the Development of Reason*, edited by Dearden, Hirst, and Peters. (*Craig writes.*) Okay? So, I realized Oakeshott was criticizing Whitehead without mentioning Whitehead's name. I suppose he could also be criticizing Dewey, but what

struck me was that he quotes Whitehead and then absolutely flays what he sees as the results. I think this is a total misunderstanding of Whitehead. Listen:

> The doctrine we are not to consider is that for all this there should be substituted an arena of childish self-indulgence . . . a place where a child may be as rude as his impulses prompt and as busy or as idle as his inclinations suggest. There is to be no curriculum of study, no orderly progression of learning. Impulse is to be let loose upon an undifferentiated confusion called, alternatively, "the seamless robe of learning" or "life in all its manifestations." What may be learned is totally unforeseen and a matter of complete indifference.

CRAIG:   Sounds like A.S. Neill's school, Summerhill. Why a criticism of Whitehead?

DAVID: Well look at what Whitehead says in *The Aims.* (*He takes a marked copy and flips it open at the first marker.*) Page 6: "There is only one subject-matter for education, and that is Life in all its manifestations." And page 11: "You may not divide the seamless coat of learning."

GLENDA: Oh! I thought those were marvelous sayings, that I had something solid to walk on there. I feel as if I am falling back into a vacuum again. Do you mean all that is nonsense after all?

DAVID: Of course not. Oakeshott is playing a game of his own, and doesn't seem to care what color he paints anyone.

HENRY: Is he? Why so sure?

DAVID: Because he's taken these passages right out of context—a context in which they point to something quite different. I'll show you. Is Whitehead encouraging self-indulgence and no guided study of subjects? No. On page 2, he says, "Do not teach too many subjects," not "don't teach any subjects." He's also clearly implying that we should certainly teach some subjects, and that we definitely should teach—not stand on the sidelines satisfied for the student to do anything he likes. And when on page 6 he says, "There is only one subject-matter for education, and that is Life in all its manifestations," he's in the middle of talking about "the fatal disconnection of subjects which kills the vitality of our modern curriculum." To criticize disconnection of subjects—artificial disconnection—is not the same as saying that all subjects are really one, that there is only one subject. I think Whitehead is distinguishing between a subject and subject-matter. He's not saying something idiotic like math is really history—or vice versa. Of course subjects are different. He is surely saying that ultimately the subject-matter—what one studies with the tools and methods of a subject—is one, namely, Life as we find it. If the subject study in education, or rather, schooling, doesn't give us any better understanding of life, what on earth is it supposed to be for? That is Whitehead's point, isn't it?

HENRY: I think so. But let's look at some details here. If the subjects are distinct, different from each other, how can they become one in relation to the one life each of us lives?

DAVID: Easily. For example, if you want to take the life of a school, with all the problems that arise and aren't supposed to, it's no good just calling on history, or just on psychology, and so on. You may need to call on history, psychology, sociology, mathematics, ethics, and even architecture.

CRAIG: I'm not sure if I understand. Do you mean that any problem of humans is complex, that any one subject or discipline can only deal with a certain type of factor, but that these complex problems are caused by many different sorts of factors?

DAVID: Yes, but not necessarily just human problems. Any real-life problem or situation. I mean, you can't understand the life of a forest just with botany. You need chemistry, physics, entomology, geology, and goodness knows what else.

HENRY: So the subjects are somewhat different, necessarily, but become one when they are together focused on the complexity of living events in order to understand them. Note that all this assumes that the overall aim of education in school is to equip students to better understand life. If that's so, the usefulness of subjects in illuminating something subtle and easily missed by uneducated observation must be made thoroughly obvious to students. Isn't that why, in one of his definitions of education on page 4, Whitehead says not that knowledge has to be acquired, but that the "art of the utilization of knowledge" has to be acquired?

CRAIG: I read Oakeshott, but it was a while ago. I thought he was opposed to the notion of education fitting people for life as it is.

HENRY: He is, if you literally mean preparing to fit people into neat slots in the existing scheme—like making square pegs for square holes. Isn't that what Oakeshott means by "socialization?" Whitehead also does not endorse that aim for schools.

DAVID: No, I think he wants schools to help students to live more intelligently, more thoughtfully, than people presently are.

LOUISE: Well, when I skimmed over some of the Oakeshott article, I got the impression that Oakeshott is putting a case rather like a skillful lawyer, exaggerating and caricaturing what he opposes in order to dramatically emphasize the points he considers fair and important. If you realize this is what he's doing, then you read him as the opposing lawyer would, and hopefully, as the judge and jury would—clearly recognizing the points on which he is unassailable, and ignoring the caricature in the presentation of the other lawyer's case. And, as said before, there's a danger in the way some teachers have misunderstood to the point of absurdity the freedom and discovery elements of all good learning. I think Oakeshott challenged David to go back to Whitehead and check him out more carefully, and as a result, David understands Whitehead better. In a way, Oakeshott has done you a service, David!

DAVID: Well, I still feel that Oakeshott is playing a dangerous game with words, and could easily give the readers such a jaundiced eye about White-head that they would never bother to read him, and that would be a great loss to them. Quite apart from the bits about subject study and curriculum, I think Oakeshott himself is missing the crucial point of Whitehead's on the effect of the right kind of interest. And the importance of the right kind of interest to the right kind of learning. Oakeshott is focusing on what knowledge is important, to the exclusion of the issue of how that knowledge is to be seen as important by any individual student. That requires interest.

ANNE: I don't dispute that Oakeshott has a style in which provocation to thought is achieved by exaggeration, but you may be misjudging him on the question of interest. Let me have your copy a minute. (*She quickly thumbs through the pages.*) Yes, this is what I was thinking of. Listen:

> If science had entered the educational engagement as an initiation into an intellectual adventure recognized as a component of an inheritance of human understanding and beliefs it would, no doubt, have constituted a benign and appropriate addition to what was already there.

CRAIG: That sounds almost ridiculous—I mean, to calmly suggest that perhaps science could have a useful place in the curriculum. How on earth could any sane teacher allow students to leave high school to make their way in a scientific/technological culture without some study of science?

ANNE: Craig, you're missing the point entirely. If you had let me finish, I was about to say that he is, like Whitehead, I believe, stating that the right use of science in the curriculum of a school which really aims to educate, must present science as it originated—as an intellectual adventure. "Adventure" means risk, excitement, interest, and so on. So in fact he does take the interest component of worthwhile learning to heart.

DAVID: All right. I concede the point. But I'm glad we have Whitehead around to treat the issue of interest as a major topic of study for educators.

CRAIG: There's something I don't understand in that Oakeshott passage. Or (*looking at Anne*) the way you interpret it. You said, "present science as it originated . . . adventure, risk, excitement," and so on. What is he implying about science as it is now?

ANNE: Well, partly reading between the lines, it is implied that science is now too much simply another profit gambit, and that influences schools to teach science in a way appropriate to earning a living as, say, an industrial scientist. In this way, science is bent into another tool for gainful employment. School science becomes just another burden of remembering piles of facts and special techniques for reasons which, to most school students, carry no immediate interest. To them, the fact that they might later be employed as scientists is boring, because it's only a possible outcome amongst others, and it seems light years away. . . . Oh, wait a minute, I'm now talking like Whitehead, not Oakeshott. I meant to say Oakeshott thinks that for the education of schools, any subject, including science, must be studied solely for its value as a manifestation of the civilized human mind at work—or perhaps play, or both. . . . I'm not sure.

CRAIG: Okay, that clears that up. But why should we criticize school education for aiming to prepare students for useful employment?

HENRY: Here I think the educational philosopher, R.S. Peters, has a helpful way of putting it—in that same collection of essays. He suggests that to get at the wisest meaning of "education" as a distinctive activity of learning and teaching, we should keep in mind that the outcome should be an "educated person," which is different from saying that the outcome should be someone with enough specialist knowledge to become a scientist with General Foods or a journalist for *The Globe and Mail*. I can guess what you're thinking, Craig. No, that doesn't mean school education should regard employability as irrelevant. What I'm getting at is the difference between seeing employability as one predictable and desirable effect of schooling, and seeing it as the governing aim of educating in school. Peters, Whitehead, and Oakeshott, too, regard "becoming an educated person" as an achievement of greater human value than merely becoming employable. Though it occurs to me, if I've become significantly educated as a person, that itself would in most cases put me in a position to find good employment.

CRAIG: I don't know what you mean by an "educated person" . . . which now strikes me as curious, since I've always assumed it was obvious.

MARIA: I think I do know what Whitehead means by an educated person. Isn't it a person with what he calls "culture," you know, "activity of thought, and sensitivity to beauty and humane feeling"?

HENRY: Plus "expert knowledge in some special direction." Yes, I would think that's his position. And it's a useful one to deal with right now. Do we want to help students merely to get jobs, especially influential ones, when in Whitehead's sense they don't have "activity of thought, and sensitivity to beauty and human feeling?"

GLENDA: I used to know a man (actually he was called Craig) who was imprisoned for resisting the draft for the Vietnam war, and when he got out he couldn't get a job anywhere. Eventually, he ended up running an underground newspaper in San Francisco, and what's really interesting is that he tried LSD, and . . . .

HENRY: Glenda, we could get quite lost if we revert to storytelling. Can you just tell us the point you have in mind and only tell enough of the story to illustrate that?

GLENDA: (*offended*) I would have thought the point was obvious. This Craig was ethical, he thought a lot about the war, he had sensitivity, humane feeling, and if that means he is educated, then becoming educated could stop you getting a job. You might even have to make a living doing something illegal. I mean, some of the things his underground paper said about the politicians was illegal slander, and his articles in favor of LSD, and against making it illegal, got him raided by the police. But he said that his experience with LSD made him a much more sensitive person than he was.

HENRY: Certainly there is no guarantee that being an educated person will ensure employment, or keep it safe once you have it. So we have to tackle the question whether for the sake of security it's better to deny a truth the educated mind reveals. Would it be better to get training in school and university as a successful businessman or industrial scientist, and not raise awkward ethical, political, spiritual, and aesthetic inquiries?

CRAIG: Wait a minute, why should we accept Whitehead's definition of "educated?" There are other definitions, it seems. Which do we choose? It all seems pretty arbitrary and subjective to me.

FRANK: Craig, congratulations. You have just recognized the tragic wisdom that our thinking is all, in the end, arbitrary, a subjective whim.

ANNE: What pathetic nonsense, Frank. Is it arbitrary whether two plus two equals four, or whether we would rather be treated with some sensitivity rather than as expendable pawns in a game?

HENRY: Before this game becomes a war, why don't we seriously consider Craig's question? I think it's a good one.

JERRY: I've forgotten what it was!

CRAIG: So have I! (*Henry waits for laughter to subside.*)

HENRY: Now I don't remember exactly what Craig asked, but it was about the choice of a definitive aim of education. Is it just a matter of personal bias, prejudice, whatever? Wasn't that it Craig?

CRAIG: That was it.

LOUISE: I think Glenda's quiet exit and certain sounds from the kitchen mean that there's fresh coffee, so why don't we take a break here and come back on that question?

There is warm agreement, and people begin to get up, stretch, and move towards the kitchen. Craig remains, looking in frustration for something he can not find in *The Aims*. After about ten minutes, Henry breaks off a private conversation he has been having with Glenda and makes for his seat. The cue starts others moving back. They settle, and the various conversations die out.

HENRY: All right, we were asking if a definitive aim for education has to be chosen arbitrarily, so that it's just a matter of either you like it or you don't. A personal preference value, if you like, instead of an objective one.

MARIA: I really can't believe that's right, but I don't know how to go about arguing it.

HENRY: Well, let's try just making up a definitive aim.

GLENDA: Where did this "definitive aim" come in? I'm not clear what you're talking about.

HENRY: What I'm getting at is the most important reason for any deliberate learning program you want to call "education" and what the most important thing is you're aiming to achieve by it.

GLENDA: That doesn't mean you only have one aim?

HENRY: No, but it means that the other aims must in some way serve that one, or in some way make sense in terms of it. For example, you might be aiming to find some pencils in class, but only because you have the more important aim to enable the children to learn to write. Or your aim in one moment might be to open some of the windows, which doesn't directly contribute to their writing, but indirectly it does, because the room is so hot it's making everyone sleepy. So you could say you have a chief, or overall, or definitive aim—an aim defining what all the activity is ultimately in the service of. Then you have subsidiary aims. And this is not just an academic point either. To be ignorant of this can have serious consequences. For example, teachers who try to keep order by fear and punishment usually don't realize that they are aiming at a kind of order which works against their other aim at good learning.

MARIA: Do you mean that if kids behave out of fear of consequences they don't learn so well because there is a bad relationship, a distance, between the teacher and student?

HENRY: Yes, that certainly, and a lot more. But I think that is enough for the moment to illustrate the point, or else we will get way off track. Am I getting tired? What was our track?

DAVID: You were going to try just making up an overall aim, to see if arbitrary personal preference is all that is, or can be, involved.

HENRY: Ah, yes. And so to see if there can be any objectivity in this choice. Well, what I mean by a definitive educational aim is an aim that makes, or should make, everything I do serve "educating." Now let's suppose that as a teacher, my definitive educational aim is to produce people who are thoughtless, know very little, guide themselves with comfortable vague slogans, are untrustworthy, and seek power and possession at any cost. Are you going to reply: "That's fine as your aim, but mine happens to be different?"

FRANK: You couldn't have a school system on that basis.

HENRY: No, because a system presupposes some important communal agreement on aim, or at least the convincing appearance of such agreement.

DAVID: It's more than that though. To your imaginary aim statement I would say something like: "Do you have any notion of what kind of a world you are helping to bring into existence? Or the conflict and tension that will be in those kids' minds when they are adults?"

HENRY: In other words, you're pointing to a common element in everyone's experience, and suggesting that this experience clearly shows some things tend to make for the best kind of life for both individuals and society, and some things tend to make for an ugly, contentious, painful, chaotic life?

FRANK: Life seems pretty ugly, painful, and chaotic already to me. I suspect those ugly things are always going to be there.

HENRY: Very likely, Frank, but there's a big difference between ugliness coming about through ignorance or mistakes, and ugliness which we cause by a sustained refusal to think deeply and responsibly about the likely consequences of our aims.

FRANK: Yes, there is. I wasn't entirely serious. What I am serious about, though, is that it might not be possible to decide or agree what the best kind of life is.

HENRY: Whether it's possible or not has to be found out. If much that is relevant to the issue really can be found out, but you take the position at the start that it can't be, obviously you won't find out because you won't try.

LOUISE: You know, I think most people don't think that one out because they find it too difficult. It is not because they think it is impossible, but that they don't know how to go about it.

HENRY: My impression is also that many people reason fallaciously from "This is an immensely difficult task" to the conclusion, "This is an impossible task." And from there it is a quick step to the practical conclusion, "Do nothing."

ANNE: Except that we can never do nothing. Our doing nothing is really repeating what we were already doing, because it is in fashion, or easy, or habitual, or familiar, or profitable. So we don't avoid responsibility by "doing nothing" because we are helping to keep the pattern in place.

FRANK: And since the boat is undoubtedly sinking, it looks foolish to blithely carry on the game of cards on deck while ignoring the increasing tilt.

MARIA: Your boat probably is sunk, Frank, but mine is not. It may have some dangerous leaks, but it's afloat and I can, and will, work on fixing the leaks.

FRANK: Bravely said by the eternal optimist. I have to admit that I do admire courage in a worthy cause.

HENRY: In that case you don't think the boat has sunk, since you obviously believe some virtues retain their merit regardless of misfortune, and that some causes can be recognized as worthy, objectively, not on account of personal whim.

FRANK: I have a nasty suspicion you may be right, though the logic of all that is a bit hazy to me at the moment. I will courageously reflect upon this worthy issue!

HENRY: While you do that, I want to know if Craig still thinks the definitive aim of education has to be an arbitrary choice, or whether it can be reasoned, to some useful extent, on the basis of the common evidence of anyone's experience.

CRAIG: No, no, I take the point. I think it's difficult and probably can't be conclusively decided, but reasoning can bring out enough of it to make the effort worthwhile. Not many people seem to think so, though, because I rarely hear people connected with education—schooling, I mean—turning that issue over together. Everyone plans and works as if the aim has been decided long ago and that everyone is guided by the same, and the right, aim.

MARIA: I agree, but all this is up in the clouds. Can we come down to earth and actually find out by dealing with some of the definitive aims Whitehead has given? So far only two have been mentioned.

GLENDA: Which two? Are there two in his book? More than two?

MARIA: We've mentioned education as "culture," you know, "activity of thought," and so on, and education as "the acquisition of the art of the utilization of knowledge." That is a mouthful! Have I got it right?

HENRY: Dead on. But what others are you referring to? This is interesting, because if you can show that he makes conflicting statements about the definitive aim, he's in deep trouble. Let's see. Where are they, Maria?

MARIA: At the bottom of page 11: "What education has to impart is an intimate sense for the power of ideas, for the beauty of ideas, and for the structure of ideas, together with a particular body of knowledge which has peculiar reference to the life of the being possessing it."

HENRY: And?

DAVID: What about pages 29 and 30, where Whitehead seems to imply that the point of education, when it's not degenerate, is to impart wisdom?

HENRY: All right, let's include that. Any others?

ANNE: Here's an embellishment on the one David spotted, on 37. Near the top he says, "its [education's] whole aim is the production of active wisdom." The addition of the "active" before "wisdom" interests me.

JERRY: The one that looked attractive to me—though how much I understand it I don't know—is on page 39. He says that "education is the guidance of the individual towards a comprehension of the art of life."

FRANK: The art of life? What is that?

JERRY: Wait, let me finish. Whitehead explains somewhat. Listen.

> And by the art of life I mean the most complete achievement of varied activity expressing the potentialities of that living creature in the face of its actual environment. This completeness of achievement involves an artistic sense, subordinating the lower to the higher possibilities of the indivisible personality. Science, art, religion, morality, take their rise from this sense of values within the structure of being. Each individual embodies an adventure of existence. The art of life is the guidance of this adventure.

FRANK: What on earth does all that mean?

LOUISE: When I first read it, I sensed it had some important meaning, but at the moment I would have to echo your question, Frank.

HENRY: What does it mean, Jerry?

JERRY: Some of the things you people seem to think are obvious, I have to sweat over; but this mystifies you, and to me it seems obvious!

HENRY: A good reason for dialogic learning, Jerry?

JERRY: Well, yes, I suppose it is, if you mean I haven't had much direct encounter with perspectives different from mine. I hadn't thought of it like that.
HENRY: Did you experience learning through dialogue at school and university?
JERRY: Not that I can remember. But it would probably have been condemned as cheating, or talking out of turn.
HENRY: So it's not really surprising that you hadn't thought about it like that, is it?
JERRY: No, I guess not.
HENRY: But anyway, tell us what the passage means to you.
JERRY: It conjures up an image in my mind of the personality as, metaphorically, a lot of empty music staff lines. Well, not completely empty. There is part of a melody written, and it might be a good one or a very poor one. And there is also a sort of repository of unused notes in the personality, snatches of tunes, interesting chords and discords, and the individual can pick and choose from these to complete, or change, the melody already started. Now he can really work at this to find out what makes the best sound, or he can listen to what he thinks is an impressive piece someone else has put together, arrange his own notes in the same way, and play it over and over. If he creates for himself and is a poor artist, his life will be boring, or a pain in the ear, or even ear-splitting. If he is a good artist, being around him will be like listening to Mozart, or Earl Hines, or perhaps Bruce Cockburn. I'm not putting them on the same level, but they are all good in their own sphere. Now if he doesn't create for himself, but chooses to copy, again his artistic sense may lead him to copy what's good or what's bad. My feeling is that even the ungifted creator is somehow superior to the copier of the best.
MARIA: Why?
JERRY: Because if he just copies, in a way he is not himself. He's a sort of musical clone. That just strikes me as a poor way to exist. I wouldn't like to discover that, apart from a few embellishments, I'm really just a copy of someone else. And then there is the vitality of creativity and the lifelessness of copying.
ANNE: You're right. When I got really depressed once and went through a course of therapy, I was horrified to discover that I was just repeating the basic patterns of parts of my parents' lives. And they were mostly patterns I really didn't like in my parents, so I was getting fed up with the way I lived, somehow feeling that a genuine "I" wasn't coming out, but not seeing any of it clearly enough to stop playing the same old tune over and over, as you put it, Jerry.
GLENDA: So what did you do, Anne? Could you change it? Did your therapist change you?
ANNE: Change me? I think you mean change the pattern that isn't me, don't you? No, of course she didn't. She didn't even try.

GLENDA: She didn't even try! Well, what kind of a therapist was she supposed to be? That doesn't make any sense to me.

ANNE: She didn't try to change me, because if she did, whose pattern would I be playing then?

JERRY: Hers. You swap one alien pattern for another.

ANNE: Exactly.

GLENDA: What is therapy, then? This doesn't make any sense to me.

ANNE: Therapy is many things, depending on who the therapist is. My therapist helped me to understand what I was doing.

FRANK: You mean she persuaded you to see yourself in terms of Freud's or Jung's or someone else's theory? That's just someone else's tune being played through you again.

ANNE: She never mentioned Freud or Jung or anyone else as far as I can remember, and certainly never handed me a theory to explain anything. There were times when I wished she had!

GLENDA: (*exasperated*) But what did she do, then? Did she do anything useful?

ANNE: She asked me questions about what I was feeling, or thinking, or why I was saying or doing what I was at that moment.

GLENDA: And did you know the answers?

ANNE: Sometimes I did, sometimes I didn't. Mostly at first I didn't, or thought I did but then realized I was trying to kid us both.

GLENDA: What did she do if you couldn't find the answer?

ANNE: It differed. Sometimes she asked a question about it from a different angle. Sometimes she left me to sit in silence until I wanted to tell her something, and sometimes we just moved on to something else.

GLENDA: Didn't she tell you if you didn't know or couldn't work it out?

ANNE: Sometimes she didn't know the answer herself. So how could she tell me? No, her attitude was that I had to see for myself whatever was true about myself, and that only if I could see it was it any good to me. Accepting what she tells me doesn't have the same effect as seeing the truth myself, directly.

GLENDA: Well, what did you need her for, then?

ANNE: Because she asked such clever questions, questions that sort of energized, woke up my mind to see what I wouldn't even have thought of looking for. Also, she was the kind of supportive friend who would stick at it with me however difficult it was and, more to the point, however difficult I was.

GLENDA: What do you mean, you were difficult? How?

ANNE: Oh, often I would get impatient, frustrated, and take it out on her. I often didn't want to look at frightening things, but she wouldn't let me parachute out, do a cute "let's talk about the weather" routine.

JERRY: And was she successful? Did you understand what you needed to?

ANNE: Yes, as a matter of fact I did understand most of it.

GLENDA: But how did understanding help you? What I mean is this: I often become aware that I'm treating the children in a bitchy way, and that it is be-

cause I have received some bad news or have had a bad day, and I would say
to myself that I wasn't going to let that happen again. But two days later I
would be at it again. Knowing what the problem was didn't seem to help me
to be different.

ANNE: It's difficult to explain, but I could try by taking over some of Whitehead's way of talking, perhaps. You see, you are aware enough to understand
that you're giving the kids heck because of the way you feel, not because of
what they are doing. But there isn't any power in that idea, because you understand too shallowly. It's virtually inert for you. No, really, I'm not being
rude. I have to face up to this in myself and so does everyone else here. If you
don't see that, you just conclude that ideas, that understanding, doesn't change
anything. You stop looking, and so of course nothing changes.

FRANK: Sounds nice, Anne, but you haven't answered the crucial question,
namely, if a deeper understanding can change things, how do you get it?

ANNE: Look, I'm not trying to make this sound like two plus two equals four.
It's difficult to describe, but there is an answer. Take the case Glenda talked
about. She would need to ask herself why, when tired or upset, she chose to
react as she did. After all, others react differently. Was it because really she
dislikes children? Or is it just a kind of program she has taken over from her
teachers when she was young, or from her mother? If she really persists, really
wants to find out, and so watches what is going on in her mind, her feelings,
when she is bitchy like that, sooner or later, she'll begin to see for herself.
Then she'll find she starts changing, acting differently without even deciding
to. This kind of understanding by direct self-observation, which is not just
speculation or second-hand theory, brings about the change. You look skeptical, as usual, Frank, but I can't prove it to you, or for you. You have to find
out for yourself if I'm right or wrong by doing it. But when that understanding
comes, it's a beautiful thing. That's why I think Whitehead is right when he
talks about the power and the beauty of ideas. When they really do represent
some important understanding for you. When they are alive, not inert. When
they give you something that matters to you.

CRAIG: I'm getting lost. We were talking about education as an art of living,
not education as experiencing the power and beauty of ideas.

LOUISE: Craig, you've just done it for me. They're the same thing. Except
that you should have said, "Education as the guiding of someone in the art of
life," not "education as the art of life."

HENRY: I think both probably have merit. But go on, Lou, explain.

LOUISE: Okay. I'm not sure I can put this intuition together in words, but I'll
have a go.

CRAIG: Before you start, I also meant to say that I'm not sure why we are
going on and on about Anne's therapist when we are supposed to be trying to
understand Whitehead on education, not to mention Jerry on the music of
education. (*His voice is drowned in laughter, and Jerry affects a haughty,
dignified injury.*)

LOUISE: For goodness sake, Craig. One thing at a time. Work out the therapy issue yourself in a minute if you want to—I'm not onto that at the moment. Now, let's see . . . . All right, look at it this way. You aren't just born an artist at living, immediately producing the greatest possible harmony and well-being and all that. You have to learn to do it, to improve the art, to even see that it is a kind of art, and an important one. If you don't get the right kind of help, you likely won't get far at all. But if you get help from someone who knows something about it, you could forge ahead by leaps and bounds. Because they can point you to the right places for the understanding you need. But to change your life to something better and more satisfying, you have to understand it, and understand it really well. Just like the painter knowing about brush strokes and color-mixing, and having the courage to paint what she really thinks is worth painting, whatever others say. Well, don't you see? Getting enough depth of understanding, and liking that process even when difficult, is what Whitehead means by experiencing the power and beauty of ideas. To be good at an art, you need a lot of interest, a lot of understanding, a lot of persistence, and . . . .

HENRY: And a strong conviction about the worth of the outcome, or intended outcome?

LOUISE: Yes. That's what I was fishing for. And my point is that at least two of Whitehead's different statements about the central aim of education are consistent with each other, perhaps the same.

CRAIG: That's all very nice, though I still don't see why we're talking about learning to live well, or live better, as an art? Why shouldn't it be a science?

HENRY: Is science an art?

CRAIG: No, well, maybe . . . yes, I suppose it is at its root. I mean that although new advances require a lot of very methodical thought and experiment, at root they are hunches, insights, intuitions . . . .

HENRY: What I seem to remember Sir Bernard Lovell called a serendipity of the mind?

CRAIG: Did he? Yes, I would agree with that. You can see it in Newton, Einstein, Kekulé, and beyond the mathematics, modern physics thrives on wild metaphors like curved space and backwards-running time.

HENRY: A kind of cosmological poetry?

CRAIG: I suppose it is. But science is also tremendously logical and analytic, and on its practical side works by very carefully set methods and routines.

HENRY: And in the crucial experimental situation, the variables are deliberately controlled, aren't they, so that its little bit of life is somewhat artificially arranged to let nothing unpredictable interfere?

CRAIG: Of course, otherwise deciding what causes what would be too much guesswork.

HENRY: I'm not criticizing the approach, just trying to see its characteristics clearly, and what its limitations are. So on the abstract side it's an intellectual art, and on its practical side it checks its theorizing within controlled environments. That's an oversimplification, of course. Now it seems to me that on both counts it can't help a movement towards wise living.

CRAIG: I think it can. It takes a scientist to tell you definitely that a substance is carcinogenic, so then you know it would not be wise to ingest it.

HENRY: Well, no you don't. The scientist, as scientist, can't tell if it would be wise to avoid that substance. He, as scientist, only tells you it's carcinogenic. You have to value life, and a healthy life, to realize it would be unwise to ingest it. To live life wisely, or intelligently, in the deep sense of intelligence, value judgments must be made, and made well. The quality of life depends on them, doesn't it?

CRAIG: Yes.

HENRY: All right, so we could say, adapting a phrase from Whitehead's *Religion in the Making*, there are the facts of life, and there is the quality of life, and while the first is the province of science, the second is not.

ANNE: It's Oakeshott who says that education is getting an understanding which illuminates the fact of life with a quality of life.

HENRY: He takes it from Whitehead! Let's see. . . . (*He picks up and thumbs through a marked copy of the 1960 Meridian Books edition of* Religion in the Making.) Yes, here on page 77 he says: "There is a quality of life which lies always beyond the mere fact of life." Now even the factual side of life is not a neatly controlled environment. It is full of unpredictability at every point. So intelligence has to have a tremendous flexibility to be true to the subtle novelty of what is happening from moment to moment. Obviously we want to use the ideas and principles of science, but the happiest or wisest application of them at any moment takes a special value awareness, which I think is much more like the artist with his peculiar sensitivity to what would be just the right touch to add next. That is why I think Whitehead is correct in talking about the art of life, not the science of life. For the same reason, I think he is right to talk about the art of the utilization of knowledge. In which case, we see that a third aim statement is consistent with the other two.

FRANK: I can go along with that, but I'm not sure why schools should see it as their function to help the student with that art.

JERRY: Frank, look at it this way. First, living is an art. Second, the students are young, impressionable. They spend a huge portion of those years in school. In one way or another how can their sense of the art of life not be affected by their schooling?

FRANK: What's your point?

JERRY: My point is that whatever you do in school is going to affect the students' grasp of the art of life, negatively or positively. So, realizing that, teachers have to think about the issue and attempt to be a positive influence.

FRANK: Why do they have to?

JERRY: Because, if through doing nothing or doing the wrong thing, or both, they help students develop a wrong view and the students mess up their own lives and the lives of those in contact with them, teachers are at least partially responsible for that. However good their intent, in effect they are careless, unprofessional, not to be trusted.

DAVID: Well look, it's right here at the end of Chapter One, where Whitehead is saying . . . wait a minute, let me find it. Yes, he's saying: "The essence of education is that it be religious. . . . Duty arises from our potential control over the course of events. Where attainable knowledge could have changed the issue, ignorance has the guilt of vice." That's it, in a nutshell. So this strange remark about education being "religious" also seems to fit in with the rest.

GLENDA: Okay, we started all this off because we wanted to know if all Whitehead's different sayings about the central aim of education are really different or somehow the same. How far have we got with that?

HENRY: Yes, Glenda, let's get back to that. I seem to remember that Lou put together the art of life and the power and beauty of ideas rather well. They seem to be aspects of the same total idea. And I think what Anne said about her understanding through therapy illustrated the way the ideas don't have power unless, as Whitehead says, they have peculiar reference to the life of the being possessing them. For that power in the ideas, Anne had to care a lot about having a transformative understanding of her situation. It became a special, I mean specialist study for her, and had to, to be effective. That's Whitehead's point about the importance of study taking some form of specialist turn of special significance to the particular individual. Not specialist in our academic sense.

CRAIG: Come to think of it, I can see that her therapist is effective, her ideas have power, because she has her own "style" and expertise through her own special study of . . . of what? Psychological, relational problems? Am I on the right track about "style"?

HENRY: Right on track, I would say, Craig.

MARIA: We've missed out what he says, what Whitehead says, in one of those aim statements about the structure of ideas. I don't understand this business about the structure of ideas.

CRAIG: Well, that's pretty clear in science. If you can't correctly connect your hypothesis ideas with your ideas about your experimentation, you are going to end up believing ridiculous things. Correct understanding requires correct structuring—connecting—of the relevant ideas.

FRANK: Same in math. Get the connections of the ideas wrong, and you end up with some complex version of two plus two equals eight!

HENRY: So you wouldn't understand, even if you thought you did. In other words, getting the connections or structure of ideas correct does determine whether your conclusion is true or false, and your practice sensible or muddled. Imagine a teacher who has the idea that students must understand for themselves, if they are to have real understanding at all. If she also still subscribes to the idea that she should tell them what to think, and can't see the inconsistency of those ideas, so getting the structure wrong, she'll wonder why her teaching doesn't encourage understanding.

MARIA: Or else she'll read parroting as understanding, and so think, wrongly, that she has been successful?

HENRY: That too.

MARIA: All right, I think I've got that.

ANNE: And although she might spout impressive theories to her colleagues about education, she wouldn't have any active wisdom when it came to teaching.

DAVID: That's nice, Anne. That fits, though we could probably leave out the "active" now, since wisdom that couldn't make action wise wouldn't be wisdom at all, would it? It would just be an intellectual caricature.

ANNE: I think we've arrived back at the beginning of the chapter, where Whitehead says a merely well-informed man is the most useless bore on God's earth, haven't we?

GLENDA: I think we've arrived at 11:15; in other words, it is late, and some of us have to teach tomorrow.

CRAIG: All right, but I for one would like to look more closely at this contrast of generalism and specialism next time.

DAVID: And I for two would like to look at the romance, precision and generalization stages of learning next time.

HENRY: I wonder if we could try something different. Craig, would you like to see if you can pull the specialism/generalism argument together for us, and you, David, do the same with the stages of learning?

Amid a good deal of banter, the rest, glad to be free of responsibility, strongly affirm that Craig and David should most definitely follow Henry's suggestion. Craig and David ruefully consider themselves volunteered. They set up a meeting place and pick and a date and time. Except for Jerry, who says he will help clear up, they all pick up their books and coats and leave.

# Six

# FOURTH DIALOGUE: DOING WHAT COMES NATURALLY

## Sunday, 3 December

By 6:30 in the evening everyone has assembled in Anne's small student apartment on campus and consumed many of the various things to eat, which she and Craig have prepared. There are some fairly intense conversations going on, and Anne needs persistence to get anyone to collect some wine, coffee, or tea and gather round for the discussion. Finally they are settled and quieting down. David is going through some pages of his journal and marking points as he goes. Craig searches anxiously for some notes, finds them, and sits down. Henry waits for complete quiet and then begins.

HENRY: I seem to remember that we were going to start by having Craig pull together the specialism/generalism issue in his own way, and David the various aspects of the romance, precision, and generalization schema of learning. Do you still want to proceed that way?
LOUISE: David does. He's done a lot of work on Chapters Two and Three. Come on, David, don't act all nonchalant. You know you really got into it. I'm a veritable journal widow! (*Embarrassed, David grins weakly and rolls his eyes to the ceiling.*)
CRAIG: Well, I'm more flexible. I'm quite open to a change of plan.
DAVID: You might be, no doubt, but if I am going to throw myself to the lions, so are you.
ANNE: It's the lionesses you'll have to watch out for.
FRANK: Before this turns into a zoo, can we get going?
HENRY: Yes, let's. Craig, do you want to start off?
CRAIG: I think David should start. I'm far too scattered at the moment after hours of menial drudgery in the kitchen under Anne's eagle eye.
ANNE: Menial drudgery? You call dipping into everything and trying it "just to make sure" menial drudgery? The eagle eye was necessary to make sure there was something left for other people!
LOUISE: You start, David. Be generous to your fellow man in distress.
DAVID: All right, but be sure you're going to be volunteered for the next one, Lou.
LOUISE: Oh, didn't I tell you that I am dropping out after this session for reasons of overwhelming housewifely duties.
FRANK: For goodness sake start, David, and do us all a favor.
DAVID: Right, I will, but Glenda, I shall need your help.

GLENDA: What?

DAVID: You piqued my interest with your remarks about Socrates, and I dipped into the *Meno* and the *Republic*. I noticed that the way Socrates conducts dialogue is different from the way we dialogue, and I'd like to see if we could do it Socrates' way. Since Socrates seems to be your hero, I'm sure you wouldn't object to answering my questions, would you?

MARIA: Would somebody mind telling me what's going on here?

HENRY: In Plato's earlier dialogues, where Socrates' questioning style is most clearly portrayed, it is apparently the custom for someone to lead with questions and someone to respond, not in the sense of supplying the answer, necessarily, but in the sense of replying in some way or another. David, this sounds interesting. Glenda, are you willing to give the replies?

GLENDA: I'll give it a try.

DAVID: Good. All right, where shall I start? Try this. When we learn anything, would you say that being able to repeat the usual words and phrases expressing the learning is the learning itself?

GLENDA: No.

DAVID: Is it true that we can repeat the usual expressions of understanding without having, to any useful degree, the understanding itself?

GLENDA: Yes.

DAVID: So that if I tell you that Paris is the capital city of France, and you didn't know that before, you could repeat that either without understanding what the statement means, or not knowing whether it is true?

GLENDA: Yes.

DAVID: Would it be true, then, to say that we can get someone to learn simply by *telling* her or him what we know, or think we know?

GLENDA: No, it wouldn't be true if it were supposed to be true all the time in any circumstances whatsoever.

DAVID: But it could be true in some circumstances?

GLENDA: Yes. For example, I might have tried everything I can to find the answer to a question, without success. Then I ask an expert in this area and she tells me. It sounds just like the right kind of answer. So I try it out, and find that indeed what she told me *is* the answer.

DAVID: All right. Now in that case, did you get the answer from her *telling* it to you, or did you get it from your own intelligence, which was active and informed from all the inquiry you had done, and therefore in a position to see for itself whether the answer given was the correct one?

GLENDA: From my own intelligence, helped by what she told me.

DAVID: Would you say, then, that you could get the answer simply or merely or only from someone telling you?

GLENDA: No. I mean, no, I couldn't.

DAVID: So even a true statement of someone else's couldn't be an answer for you? That is, you could not recognize it as the conclusion, unless you had already done the work of understanding language and seeing what sort of things could not be the answer to your question?

GLENDA: Yes, that's what I mean.

DAVID: Well, it seems then that we don't come to learn, or understand, by being told. Now if to learn, to understand, means to recognize the meaning, importance and truth of something, how do we come to learn?

GLENDA: By exercising our intelligence, I suppose.

DAVID: And would we recognize someone exercising his or her intelligence by noting whether learning occurred?

GLENDA: Yes, I would say so.

DAVID: In that case, do we recognize the occurrence of learning by noting the exercise of intelligence, and recognize the exercise of intelligence by noting the occurrence of learning?

ANNE: Oh, that's tricky. You have her going round in a circle!

HENRY: And so getting nowhere. Do you see that, Glenda?

GLENDA: Yes, but I don't see how I got trapped into that.

HENRY: David?

DAVID: Try responding to my question about how we come to learn, without talking about the exercise of intelligence. You see, we already defined learning as the exercise of intelligence. Where, for example, does learning begin for you?

GLENDA: The learning of anything?

DAVID: Yes.

GLENDA: I suppose, if what we are doing now is an example, I begin learning by being asked a question I don't already know the answer to.

DAVID: Does one necessarily have to be asked a question?

GLENDA: No, not necessarily. I might just hit on it by myself.

DAVID: You might ask yourself a question?

GLENDA: Yes.

DAVID: And how then did you learn enough language to ask a question, or else, how did you learn anything before you could use speech?

GLENDA: Oh, heavens! What are you all smiling at? All right, David, I'll answer. I used my senses.

DAVID: And by that you mean your sight, hearing, and so on?

GLENDA: Of course!

DAVID: So you would say we learn sometimes by the senses and sometimes by asking a question?

GLENDA: Yes. Though when we ask a question we are using what we get from our senses.

DAVID: Shall we look at the case of learning by using the senses but having no question?

GLENDA: If you want to.

DAVID: Well, I do, because it seems very puzzling to me.

GLENDA: I don't see anything puzzling about it.

DAVID: Let's consider an infant without any language sufficient for having a question. Clearly, he learns a great deal, including how to ask questions. You say he learns all this by using his senses. Now I wonder, are the senses enough? If I see something—I mean, just having my eyes trained in a certain direction—what do I get simply by virtue of using my eyes? What does the eye alone give me?

GLENDA: Oh, I see what you mean. Just the eye with no thinking or feeling, or anything like that?

DAVID: Yes.

GLENDA: Colors, shapes.

DAVID: Right. And if I use the ears alone?

GLENDA: Sounds. And you don't need to go through all the senses. I can see that the answer would be similar in each case.

DAVID: All right. So if for simplicity we just use, say, three senses—sight, hearing and touch—can you imagine the predicament of the infant trying to learn all sorts of necessary things with only a mixture of colors, shapes, sounds and feels? How would such mixtures become "mother," "chair," "hot stove," and so on? Would any such mixture of sense impressions organize itself into units with constant meaning?

GLENDA: Of course not. The infant organizes them.

DAVID: But you said the infant uses only the senses to learn. You didn't say anything about the capacity to organize into units with constant meaning.

GLENDA: Oh, okay. I assumed that. So the infant has this organizing capacity. We need to be able to organize our sense impressions into meaningful units to be able to learn.

DAVID: What if the infant didn't want to, or couldn't be bothered to put in the effort to organize, and reorganize, until he gets things right? Then he won't learn, presumably, will he?

GLENDA: But infants do learn.

DAVID: Then would we be right to say that they need adequate motivation to put in the effort?

GLENDA: Yes, yes. They would need to be adequately motivated.

DAVID: And what kind of thing would definitely motivate an infant, or anyone, to learn?

GLENDA: I have no idea. Don't they have all kinds of motivation?

DAVID: Well, let's see. Take the case of the infant touching a hot stove for the first time. What would motivate him to learn not to touch it?

GLENDA: The heat . . . , I mean, the pain.

DAVID: If it was pleasurable, he would probably want to touch it again?

GLENDA: Very likely, yes.

DAVID: Which of these constitutes a problem for him, pleasure or pain?

GLENDA: Pain, obviously. Since when is pleasure ever a problem?

DAVID: Well, that might make an interesting inquiry! But to keep to the example, for the moment, would you say that he learns not to touch primarily because of the pain itself, or because pain presents a problem to him?

GLENDA: Both, I'd say.

DAVID: Do you mean that the pain would be enough to activate his learning, without it seeming to be a problem of some kind?

GLENDA: No, no. It would have to feel like a problem, otherwise children would burn themselves to death before they learned.

DAVID: So which is of primary importance for motivating, for activating, learning: there being a pain, or there being the sense of a problem of some sort?

GLENDA: I suppose the sense of there being a problem must be primary.

DAVID: And is the kind of problem we are talking about a problem of not knowing something we feel a strong need to know? In the case of our infant, not knowing about stoves and their danger to him?

GLENDA: The problem for him might be not knowing how to get relief for the pain, or comfort from someone.

DAVID: Agreed. But it would still be a problem of not knowing something he feels a need to know?

GLENDA: Yes.

DAVID: Our infant, then, even without language, can nonetheless learn because he can feel the presence of the problem of not knowing something he needs to know?

GLENDA: Yes.

DAVID: And when you, having language, ask a question to help your learning, is that question the outcome of the same feeling of having a problem of not knowing something you need to know? Or is it the outcome of something else?

GLENDA: No, it's the outcome of feeling I need to know something—what you said first.

DAVID: You said earlier that your learning begins with the asking of a question. Would you now still say that, or would you say that your learning begins with the sense of a problem of not knowing something you need to know?

GLENDA: Oh, I see where you're going. All right, I would have to say that the sense of the problem of not knowing something comes first. I mean, when you do have language, what would the question be about otherwise?

DAVID: Precisely. And this often vague but powerful sense of there being a problem of not knowing something one needs to know, would you say that this is or is not one of the stages of real learning that Whitehead mentions? You know, "romance," "precision," or "generalization."

GLENDA: I think . . . , I'm sure it would be the romance stage of learning, because he describes that as a stage where one gets an exciting feeling of something new to understand. (*She begins to smile as she suddenly understands the point of David's questioning.*)

DAVID: So then would you say that Whitehead is right when he insists that the romance stage is the initial stage of real learning, and that the learning will not be real learning, or the important kind of learning, if the romance stage is not the initial stage?

GLENDA: I would say he is definitely right. (*David laughs as some of the group voice their approval of his Socratic style of questioning. Henry, Maria, and Jerry even begin to clap.*)

HENRY: Well done, David. I take my hat off to you. I must admit I wondered if you knew what you were doing, but you've proved that you certainly did. I do believe Socrates would definitely approve, had he been here.

LOUISE: David, I never knew you had it in you. I'm impressed. You'd make us a lot of money as a lawyer.

DAVID: Oh Lou, what a backhanded compliment, associating philosophic inquiry with the sophistry of law courts!

MARIA: What is sophistry?

FRANK: The clever art of appearing to prove anything you like, whether it is true or not.

MARIA: Well, then, I don't think that was sophistry. I think David was doing something else . . . philosophy, I suppose. But something else is becoming clear for me, too. You see, I would have gotten tied up in the same places Glenda did. And I now realize why.

HENRY: Why, Maria?

MARIA: Because I hadn't thought "learning" through completely, and so I didn't really understand why Whitehead insists that learning must start in a romance stage. But now it's quite clear.

GLENDA: Well, it's clear to me now that much learning does start with a romance stage, but I'm not sure it has to. Much of the learning in school does not.

MARIA: But won't the students end up with inert ideas otherwise?

GLENDA: Perhaps, but I don't see why.

MARIA: It's because what the teacher says or asks doesn't relate to any sense of a problem for the students. The teacher may see a problem, but the students don't. So they don't see any point in doing the learning. They aren't really learning, they're just remembering, if they can, what the teacher is doing with words...or numbers. You have to have a strong sense of yourself not knowing something you really need or want to know before your intelligence is active enough to begin to organize ideas into something personally meaningful. Otherwise, what is it that Whitehead says? (*She thumbs through* The Aims *and quickly stops at page 9.*) Here it is. Listen: "The pupils have got to be made to feel that they are studying something, and not merely executing intellectual minuets." Wait! Yes, now Henry, you have to keep your promise to answer, because I think I know why you refused to give me, us, little summaries of Whitehead's point of view when we began the dialogues.

HENRY: My promise is still good. Why did I refuse?

MARIA: Because we wouldn't have started understanding Whitehead on education at the romance stage, and so if you'd told us everything you thought, we would very likely have ended up with inert ideas about Whitehead! You would have started at a precision stage. Am I right?

HENRY: Completely so. Nice going. I am unmasked. But whose stage of precision would it have been anyway? Mine or yours?

MARIA: Well, yours, I suppose. Yes, it wouldn't even have been our precision stage.

HENRY: Exactly. It wouldn't have expressed anything you, and you alone, had begun to understand in a precise, exact, ordered way. Now do you forgive me?

MARIA: Most completely, kind sir.

JERRY: "To understand all, is to forgive all."

GLENDA: That's nice. It's Whitehead, isn't it?

JERRY: Not exactly. It's a French proverb he quotes on page 2.

GLENDA: I knew I'd read it in there somewhere.

CRAIG: Wait a minute, I have a question now. Is Whitehead's point also that we are in need of the precision stage, coming second, after romance, if we are not to end up with inert ideas? And does the generalization stage necessarily have to come third?

DAVID: Yes.

CRAIG: Why?

DAVID: Suppose you have a vague, strong sense of a problem—or even of a possible solution to a problem, and it's one that you care a lot about. It's still all vague. What can you do with that? You can't use it to understand anything. You don't know clearly enough what "it" is.

CRAIG: All right. So if you don't find a way to make it precise, you can't use if for anything—you can't share it, apply it, test it, prove it, or anything. You can't "generalize" it. Is that it?

DAVID: Yes. And even if you had got it precise, what would happen if you missed out the generalization stage?

CRAIG: You wouldn't use it.

DAVID: Exactly. All that effort at getting it precise for nothing! If you did that too many times you would stop bothering. You would be turned off learning!

HENRY: And you might become a bumptious pedant, always demanding clarity and precision and exactitude for no useful purpose that anyone can see.

FRANK: I'd like to see if I have something precise here or not. As I understand from what's been said, Whitehead means that it's natural to intelligence to go about learning by starting with a romance stage and proceeding through to a generalization stage. I mean natural in the sense that to try to learn, to really understand, any other way—or to be forced to—would be like trying to get one's knee joint to bend the other way. Is that right?

LOUISE: What a revolting analogy, Frank.

FRANK: Perhaps it ought to be for what we are talking about. (*He looks at David.*) But anyway, I was addressing our resident expert on the differences between the stages of romance, precision, and generalization.

DAVID: Kneecapped by school, eh, Frank?

LOUISE: You two are perverse.

DAVID: Seriously, Frank, my impression is that Whitehead means exactly what you said. His three stages are a way of pointing out the only way intelligence can work, if it works at all.

FRANK: Right. Well, let's see if I understand "generalization," now I have that idea precise, by doing some generalization. I understand generalization to mean understanding an idea in such a way that it can apply to many more things than were apparent at the romance stage. Am I on track?

DAVID: Yes, I believe so.

FRANK: Then I want to generalize this idea about the stages being the natural way intelligence works. If this is true, then one of Whitehead's criticisms of schooling is that too much teaching is done in a way that hinders the natural working of intelligence, and this is why there must be so much failure. Is that right?

HENRY: What sort of failure, Frank?

FRANK: Oh, I know that students pass exams and get jobs and go to university. But as I now see it, they can do all that and still just be doing clever tricks with inert ideas. If you really challenged them to think hard with those ideas you'd find how shallowly they were understood.

HENRY: Yes, I'm sure you're right. But how would you describe the kind of failure you're hinting at?

FRANK: Hah! You want me to get this idea to the precision stage?

HENRY: You said it. Is it worth it to you?

FRANK: Yes, it is, because my job of teaching is beginning to warm up with a sense of nice possibilities to lift me out of the rut I've fallen into. So, precisely what sort of failure? Well, failure to develop the capacity for understanding, beyond that required to slip through a few school routines. Yes, so it's failure to develop the capacity for understanding. That sounds bad enough to me for a school that's supposed to be educating, and I accuse myself here, too.

ANNE: There's also the failure of turning people off understanding altogether, so that they think serious talk is still just talk, an inquiring mind is a pretentious or a strangely over-serious disposition, the reading of good, and often difficult books is tiresome, and so on. It's all a kind of mindlessness, and that is tragic. To really think is considered "academic"—like a kind of disease. I get that from other students if they discover I'm enjoying a paper I'm writing. It's as if they think I'm enjoying a broken arm or a forty mile run.

JERRY: There's another side to that, too. Anyone who persists at a difficult task of playing an instrument, composing, or writing . . . .

DAVID: Writing a journal?

LOUISE: Don't answer that, Jerry.

JERRY: I won't. I steer the peaceful course. All I was saying was that I think too many people leave school and university unable to grasp what could motivate anyone to persist for years at something difficult, quite willingly. So that serious artists, for example, are to them a mystery. And that's a tremendous loss to them, because they never themselves experience one of the best things life has to offer, I mean, finding and persisting at what you really love to do. And I think I can now see why. If you've been required for years, without much choice, to do difficult things that are rather meaningless, you must get the impression that anything difficult is drudgery. But if your heart is in it, although it may be difficult, it's not drudgery.

HENRY: I think what you say is beyond question, Jerry. So there's the failure of not having our capacity to understand developed, the failure of learning to detest learning, and the failure of never finding that hard work at what you love to do is a very precious thing in life. Just the failure to find what it is you deeply love to do strikes me as serious enough for separate mention. Without that, I'd say life is drudgery, interspersed with brief flashes of superficial entertainment. Whitehead's emphasis on "enjoyment" is a reminder of the tragedy of all this.

ANNE: And you know what I would call those kinds of failure, if they are all put together? Failure to educate. In that case, the very thing for which I would think schools should exist, they tend to fail in.

CRAIG: This is going too fast for me. First Frank pointed out that Whitehead's three stages are supposed to capture the way learning naturally happens if someone doesn't distort it. Then, if I remember, Frank said he thought too much of teaching does go against this natural grain of learning, and the result is, must be, a failure to develop the student's capacity for understanding. That's an educational failure; I can see that. But being turned off learning altogether? I'm not sure about that. I know plenty of people who have hated school, and I can see their reasons. But they have enjoyed learning how to pursue a trade, to run a business, to ski down black runs, and all that.

LOUISE: I can see what you mean, Craig. But I think what Anne, at least, was getting at was the enjoyment of learning all sorts of things that make life richer, give it more meaning. Things like literature, art, philosophy. Not necessarily things that make you any money, or give you high status, or earn you a living, or give some exciting but short-lived pleasure.

CRAIG: Well, I can't help feeling there is something snobbish about that. I suspect that literature, art, and philosophy could only ever be enjoyed in the way you are suggesting by people from very privileged backgrounds.

ANNE: Oh, heavens above, Craig! Have you never heard of wise people, artists, writers, and inventors coming from backgrounds of poverty, squalor, bare survival? And many of the people I've met from privileged backgrounds are only familiar with the surface of literature, art, and philosophy. They don't really care about it any more than anyone else, except as a sort of upper-class

*Doing What Comes Naturally*

conditioning which makes them think it's "good taste" to be around the edges of such stuff. Don't you think it is partly the fault of schools that literature, art and philosophy could still be regarded as snobbish pursuits of the privileged? If schools had been really successful for the last forty years, wouldn't most people now know that literature, art, and philosophy can enrich the life of anyone who can read, who has been given a chance to explore them in a meaningful way? I mean, if they had been encouraged to take their own artistic and philosophic moments seriously and shown how to take them somewhere useful?

HENRY: I don't doubt there is much in what you say, Anne, though to be certain of it would take considerable time with history, sociology and so on. We can certainly say we are acquainted with too much schooling that proceeds as if educational theorists like Whitehead had never spoken; and we can note that many of the essays in *The Aims* have been in print since 1917.

ANNE: (*She has been half-listening and trying to find something in one of the books she has brought.*) Look Craig, here is the kind of mistake I think you're making. Anthony O'Hear is criticizing the idea that "...only the minority who are capable of academic excellence are really capable of benefiting from a study of the works of high culture." Then he says that of course only a few people achieve excellence, by definition, but that's no reason why the majority should be thought incapable of gaining much that is valuable from such study. O'Hear shows that there is confusion over the term "elite." He says:

> Although the activities of high culture have their own standards of excellence, and hence their own elite, there is no *a priori* reason to suppose that a member of a cultural elite (such as a top physicist) has also to be a member of a social elite, nor that the majority of the population are incapable of deriving any benefit from an acquaintance with at least some of the works of the cultural elite.

CRAIG: What is that book?

ANNE: *Education, Society, and Human Nature*—it's recent, 1981. (*She hands it to him open at page 153.*)

CRAIG: Thanks. (*He scans the passage.*) Well, all right, I see the point. We could find many members of a cultural elite, like physicists, who are not and never have been members of a social elite like the upper classes. Nonetheless, I also know that a great deal of teaching of the works of "high culture"—Shakespeare, for example—seems to be quite wasted. For a start, it's too culturally different in language for many students to relate to it.

MARIA: What you high school teachers could learn from looking at elementary schools is that the so-called academic subjects do not have to be taught in a mountain of abstract lectures and exhausting note-taking. Shakespeare can be acted, and translated into the language and scenes of modern life, portrayed in really good movies, and painted, and so on. You don't have to limit yourselves to academic literary criticism to convey something of the marvel of Shakespeare. You could do some imaginative teaching!

HENRY: I agree with the point in general, Maria, though I don't want to take sides in an elementary school versus high school debate. As a matter of fact, what you said reminded me of the fine work of Dorothy Heathcote in educating through improvised drama. I have seen videos in which she shows that this can be done whether the area of study be largely historical, literary, scientific, or whatever. One thing her work represents, whether she has read Whitehead or not, is that she has a superb grasp of the importance of the romance stage of learning, and how it can be accommodated in schools with practically all kinds of students.

GLENDA: I'm getting confused here. This "high culture" you've been talking about, this is not what Whitehead refers to as "culture," is it? I mean, in Whitehead's sense, if you are "cultured," through proper education, you have "activity of thought, sensitivity to beauty and humane feeling." And this doesn't require much exposure to great works of art in school or elsewhere.

HENRY: Yes, I think that's true, though I suspect the teachers would have been influenced by great works. Nonetheless, don't you think immersion of the right kind in great works of one kind or another would greatly help Whitehead's "culture" of mind? As you've probably read, Whitehead has some interesting things to say about this in Chapter Four, "Technical Education and Science and Literature." But take care, Glenda, when mentioning education and exposure in the same breath, because your phrase "exposure to" great works carries a dangerous meaning. If you are exposed to something, it touches you only on the outside, so to speak. Like getting a short-lived sun tan. But in school, as we have seen, exposure of that kind leads to inert ideas. That's why I prefer to speak of "immersion." It implies getting deeply into something, so that it does not become inert. I quite like R.S. Peters's phrase "initiation into," as well. Though he tends to confuse things by also talking of the "transmission" of worthwhile knowledge.

MARIA: Why is that a confusion?

HENRY: Similar problem to "exposure." Can I literally transmit or give directly to you an appreciation of Shakespeare which will significantly illuminate some part of life for you? I mean, in the sense that I can give you a book?

MARIA: No, but that's obvious to anyone, isn't it?

HENRY: No, I'm afraid it isn't. We've already talked at length about teachers commonly assuming that they can give, in words, all sorts of knowledge to students. And we have agreed that what happens is that the students get very little other than the words. That is . . . .

MARIA: They don't get the understanding, the meaning that changes their way of seeing life. Yes, I remember. So you're suggesting that using the word "transmit," like "exposure," can get one into trouble in practice?

HENRY: That's exactly it. "As we think, we live." And I'm also uncomfortable with O'Hear saying "an acquaintance with at least some of the works of the cultural elite." Having "an acquaintance with" suggests something too shallow, like a sudden breeze on my face. When it's gone there's no effect left.

LOUISE: Aren't we getting a bit off track?

HENRY: Not really. Why would 'Whitehead feel it necessary to emphasize over and over that learning of any useful depth and personal significance will and must proceed as his three-stage schema suggests? Because of the universal power of these ways of speaking and thinking which imprison the mind in an iron-clad caricature of understanding.

LOUISE: All right. Well, I have a question in my notes, about romance, precision, and generalization. Is it appropriate to raise it now?

FRANK: Yes, let's get back to that.

LOUISE: My overall impression from Chapter Two was that the romance, and other stages of learning are associated with age periods from infancy to adulthood. Whitehead says that the first great stage of romance in learning is naturally in what we would call middle childhood—roughly eight to twelve. And then there are age periods corresponding to a big precision stage, and a generalization stage. But then Whitehead also says that the infant's process of acquiring language is also a complete cycle of romance, precision, and generalization. He also talks of the stages coming at different times for different subjects, like science. I'm getting lost in all that. Either he's confused, or I'm not seeing the picture whole.

DAVID: Well, I'm coming to see it as quite simple. I'll do what Whitehead suggests and apply it to you, so that it has personal meaning, and then the general meaning may become clearer. At what stage is our understanding of Whitehead's characterization of learning by stages?

LOUISE: A romance stage. Because I find it pretty interesting, and it's vague, it's not precise. I haven't thought of learning like that before, and I sense, vaguely, that it suggests some important changes in teaching, or parenting children, or living as a whole, for that matter.

DAVID: Ah, that's interesting. You see, part of your romance interest is already coming out of the anticipation of a generalization stage—how and where to use it. So in actual learning the stages are not neatly separated. One stage is dominant, but the others are there. The precision stage . . . .

LOUISE: Yes, the precision stage is coming for me; I can see that. My question was itself a desire to move into a more precise understanding of the stages. So I'd now say I was partly at the romance stage, partly at the precision stage, with the precision stage becoming dominant, right?

DAVID: Yes, that sounds right.

CRAIG: All right, Lou, but where are you in relation to learning about black hole physics?

LOUISE: Black hole physics? I don't know. I don't know what a black hole is in physics. I'm not even interested.

CRAIG: Okay. So with the subject of black hole physics you aren't even ready for the romance stage of understanding it. You're not interested.

LOUISE: No.

CRAIG: All right, if I tell you that there are volumes in space where matter is trapped by immense gravitational force, so that only what had a velocity greater than the speed of light could escape, how does that make you feel?

LOUISE: As if I am listening to a foreign language. I got a brief feeling of curiosity, but mostly it just seems irrelevant.

CRAIG: Yes, because you have to know a lot of physics before you could see anything interesting in that statement. But you don't know the physics. Can't you imagine a child of, say, seven, being perplexed in the same way by talk of even simple kinds of scientific method? Suppose the teacher said: "We don't know why the boiling point of water alters with air pressure and elevation above sea level. Let's form a hypothesis, and test it. What will we need?" It's meaningless to the child. So the child is not ready even for the romance stage of science.

DAVID: But that child may have long reached a generalization stage in writing. I mean, she might be writing letters to friends, or writing stories of her own, or leaving messages for family members. Lou, what stage are you at in cooking, or classifying and compiling legal documents?

LOUISE: Cooking? Generalization stage, I suppose, because I invent and modify dishes with the understanding I've acquired from following recipes, seeing how cooking techniques work out, and so forth. Legal documents? Again, the—or should I say a—generalization stage, for similar reasons. But as to presenting a case in court, as a lawyer does, I'm only in a romance stage. I have a vague sense of how it goes, but if I was called on to do it, I'd quickly look rather foolish.

HENRY: That's good. So you can see what Whitehead means by "cycles within cycles," where continuing through romance to generalization in any learning is one cycle. Learning to speak in sentences is a cycle lasting, say, two years. Whereas learning to be an adult takes at least twenty years. And you are ready for the romance of learning to speak when only weeks or months old, because that's what you want to do, and because it's a task you do have the ability to start. But at six, you aren't interested in learning about grammar, you don't see the point of it, and you aren't capable of the kind of reasoning required. So for grammar, you aren't ready at six even for the romance stage of learning about grammar.

LOUISE: Though the six-year-old can use grammar, or else she wouldn't be able to speak, or write her stories, or whatever.

HENRY: Yes. Isn't that intriguing, being able to use or do something you've learned, but not being able to explain what it is you do? Like learning to ride a bike.

FRANK: What's intriguing for me is your stamina. It's 8:15, I'm dying for a cup of coffee, and poor old Craig hasn't said a word about specialism and generalism.

HENRY: You're right, Frank. I'd completely lost track of time. Shall we break and then see if we have any energy for a brief word from Craig?

There is general agreement. Anne and Craig make for the kitchen, others stand and stretch. There is a yawn or two, and Frank hangs out of the open window exaggeratedly filling his lungs with fresh oxygen. Anne shoos Craig off to look at his notes, and she and Louise start pouring coffee. After about fifteen minutes, Henry asks if everyone has had enough, or if they want to hear from Craig. Craig immediately says he is much too tired and is drowned in cries for his "party piece."

HENRY: It looks as though you are an irresistible orator in overwhelming demand, Craig. Can you possibly disappoint the masses in the face of such enthusiasm?

DAVID: Of course he can't. Come on, Craig, enlighten us all. Or at least inspire us.

CRAIG: Okay, okay. I think I'll start with the idea of what is "natural." Whitehead is saying, just like the three stages of learning, that specialism is natural. Which means that if you block it, as a teacher, you're in trouble and so is the student. I find that interesting, because when I was in school I was told at various times, in effect, that I had to specialize in printing, and in long division, and then in sciences rather than arts, and none of it felt natural to me. In fact it usually turned me off. I wanted to do something else. So Whitehead doesn't mean being forced to specialize in this or that. He means that, when unhindered, intelligence always goes in a direction special to the individual. At one time, we want to learn to walk, and that's the big interest. Then we want to use the dress-up clothes in kindergarten, and the teacher says we can't—it's painting time. Later we want to date girls, or boys, and parents and teachers say we must do homework. Maybe they're right. I'm not sure, but the point is, we always have some special kind of learning we want to do at any time, so specialism is natural.

GLENDA: I thought specialism was specializing in a particular subject, like math, or languages.

CRAIG: Well, it can be, but it's more than that. You can be specializing in a particular task, or topic, or subject area. The essential idea of Whitehead's is simply that the important and natural specialism is what you really want to do, keep doing, and do well, at any time. And if teachers force a special task, they don't get special interest, and so not much of any value is learned or understood. The student is resisting, doing only the minimum to get by.

LOUISE: But if teachers allow children to just specialize in what happens to interest the children, won't their learning be very narrow? What about "general culture," where you know some useful things in all sorts of areas?

CRAIG: Look, Whitehead is not an advocate of children doing whatever they like. He makes that clear over and over. He is an advocate of the art of teaching, I mean, teaching with the care needed if you are going to succeed in educating. For example, part of that art is seeing a way to fire the interest of the student, so that a romance stage of learning begins. This is a romance stage which would not have begun without the teacher. After all, school presumably exists because in day-to-day life most children would not learn all sorts of things they need to know. Often they are not even aware that they need to know them. So the teacher is there to evoke their awareness of these things, to bring out the interest and importance as something the children immediately feel and then to guide the children in really making something of the learning.

LOUISE: I still don't see how "general culture" comes out of this. I see a lot of interesting bits and pieces coming out of it.

CRAIG: Whitehead says something really good on this on page 11. He says:

> The general culture is designed to foster an activity of mind; the specialist course utilizes this activity . . . in the general course foci of special interest will arise; and similarly in the special course, the external connections of the subject drag thought outwards. One of the ways of encouraging general mental activity is to foster a special devotion.

Now whether this can happen in school depends on the teacher, and how well he understands that both are needed, and why, and how he might go about it. But the point is straightforward, or so it seems to me. Take as an example science teaching. The teacher may have stirred some interest in electricity with some fascinating stories from the history of the discovery of electricity—lightning, static electricity, whatever. And perhaps he has given one or two demonstrations. Now he puts all sorts of things at their disposal—batteries, wires, different kinds of objects, some of which conduct, some of which don't—and he encourages the students to play around to see what they can do and find out. A science educator, David Hawkins, calls this the "messing around" stage. And not everyone in the class may be doing this at the same time. So then the teacher talks with them about what they have found out, asks them questions, perhaps shows them how to start their own books about what they've done. Then he begins to show them what some famous discoverers have found out with this kind of apparatus. Do you see? Already their thinking is being dragged outward into history, math, chemistry. Now one student might be really interested in some historical discovery about this, while another might want to go into the ways that batteries work. So the teacher lets them specialize according to interest in one aspect or another of the subject. It doesn't matter if they don't learn it all. Who ever does? The main thing is that they are learning to inquire, think, write, draw, read, make practical things, talk it over with each other, and at the same time getting a good idea of what science is and how one goes about it. I'm not sure where to go from here, except to say that I imagine what Hawkins calls the "messing around" stage is at least one way of having a romance stage of learning here, isn't it?

MARIA: I like this. Who is Hawkins?

CRAIG: (*He looks at his notes.*) David Hawkins, a philosophy professor at Colorado, who was director of the Elementary Science Study for a while. I found his article, "Messing About in Science" in the February 1965 issue of *Science and Children.*

HENRY: Let's talk about what you have here so far, before we move anywhere else. You've given an example of the way the general subject of electricity can generate specialist studies for individual students, and how, at the same time, this is being done so that all kinds of other subjects are worked with, and so that the general capacity to inquire into and think about *anything* is further developed.

FRANK: That sounds like the "transfer of learning." I've read that some people think that can't happen, because there's a different kind of thinking for different areas of knowledge.

HENRY: To some extent I think that's true. It's hard to imagine how the intuitive thinking involved in learning to paint through practice could somehow help your skill in algebra. But in other ways it can happen, and this has been demonstrated. I remember how, for me, learning to think philosophically, which requires very disciplined thought, was greatly helped by having learned to pursue a scientific inquiry. And then in my literature classes I was finding more in some of the epic poems and novels than the professor, because she wasn't sensitive enough to the philosophic innuendoes of what the writers were doing. That doesn't mean that philosophy is literary analysis, or that science is philosophy, or vice versa. There are just some aspects of thinking and inquiry that they have in common. If the teacher can highlight these for the student, the student then begins quite naturally applying these ways of thinking and inquiry in other areas. That's very much what the generalization stage is about: finding general principles and generalizable techniques in some special study you have been doing and learning how to use them in quite different areas.

DAVID: So Whitehead's "general culture" is closely related to his stage of generalization, even if it's not the same thing?

CRAIG: And in a different way, it's closely related to the romance stage, since the materials of general culture can be used to spark all sorts of new interest and a sense of new horizons, always depending on how the teacher introduces the ideas and the materials. But what we haven't emphasized is that you can't get deeply enough into the special study to find generalizable ideas unless you have an adequate precision stage. This is where I see the discussion of "style" coming in. You can't develop your own style—where you're at your best and working in the way most satisfying and effective for you—unless you've done tremendously persistent precision work. And I don't think the style, which is unique to the individual, could come if you didn't have your own special interest in the work. Also, without the interest you wouldn't persist enough. I suppose this is what you were getting at earlier, Jerry. Or at least, that was the way I was interpreting what you were saying about developing persistence and finding its rewards.

JERRY: Yes, that's what I was after.

CRAIG: Okay, I was going somewhere, but I can't remember where.

DAVID: Perhaps I can come in here, because you've made me realize I forgot to mention the importance of freedom and discipline in all this. Your example of science teaching and what you said about style and precision show exactly what I think Whitehead is saying about freedom and discipline. In the romance stage, and also in the generalization stage, we need considerable freedom to play around with things and ideas, in order to discover, to find new applications. The teacher would have to encourage us to follow our own noses, with appropriate guiding and questioning suggestions here and there. But for the precision stage we have to be very disciplined to get things clear, through discussion, practice, reading books on the topic, and so on. I don't mean "discipline" in the usual sense, you know, to discipline someone else who is thought to be lazy or troublesome. I mean that we have to discipline ourselves in order to get anything definite and worthwhile out of what we have been exploring.

FRANK: The problem is right there. Students are so unwilling to be disciplined in their work. They would leave it in a shoddy state with all sorts of loose ends if allowed to.

JERRY: But surely, Frank, that's because they haven't been helped to find any interest in the work. Of course we don't want the hard work of disciplined study and practice if we can't see any point in it. But anyone who is really interested is quite naturally prepared to work very hard at it, because when you are interested even hard work is still something like play.

GLENDA: I agree with that. Time and again I see that children who have got really interested in a topic are prepared to put unbelievable effort into what they're doing. They don't need to be disciplined to it by someone else. The difficulty is in getting them to stop and rest, have a meal, refresh themselves for a while with some different kind of activity.

FRANK: You mean you see the so-called problem of discipline as really being a problem of a lack of the right kind of interest?

GLENDA: Yes, I suppose I do, though that might be a bit oversimplified. I mean, often teenagers or adults have never, since early childhood, been allowed or encouraged to find their interest in something and pursue it. So they get a sort of habit of thinking that all self-disciplined effort is something to be escaped if possible. I'm not sure how I would deal with that attitude. The younger children I teach are almost always ready to try something new, if it seems to have some interest, even if they have had some bad experiences with former teachers. Overall, Frank, when have you ever seen someone causing trouble endlessly if they are really interested in getting something done?

FRANK: I've seen students really interested in causing trouble endlessly!

MARIA: That's just being tricky, Frank. And are adults any different? You know what Glenda means. Your troublesome students are only finding interest in being a pain because they're bored and frustrated. And they are extremely self-disciplined in causing disruption, you have to admit. So really you have admitted Glenda's point that sufficient interest supplies the willingness to be persistent, to be self-disciplined. If you can't interest them in the subject you teach, I'd say that's your problem.

ANNE: I warned you that it would be the lionesses you would have to worry about around here. I think you've been hunted down to earth, Frank. Are you ready to give up the struggle against overwhelming odds?

FRANK: "Odds" is a very good way to describe some people round here! Good heavens, if these were overwhelming odds for me, I would have expired as a result of my school problems years ago.

MARIA: Perhaps you did, but didn't notice it.

FRANK: Now I do notice a claw mark! I vote we abandon persistence and take the easy way out—out the door and home to bed.

LOUISE: All right, all right children! Please! I am tired, and I am willing to give Frank a dignified way out.

FRANK: A sister of mercy present . . . .

LOUISE: Seeing that he can't face up to the truth!

FRANK: Oh, my mother! A wolf in sheep's clothing.

DAVID: Frank, would you like to lead off with something next time we meet?

FRANK: As a matter of fact I had something I wanted to talk about tonight, something that happened last week in my class at school. I could talk about that.

HENRY: Shall we also have Chapter Four, "Technical Education, Science and Literature," ready to discuss?

It is agreed that the next Sunday they will meet at Frank's house and that this will be the last meeting before Christmas. As others leave, Anne, Craig, and Jerry start cleaning up.

# Seven

# FIFTH DIALOGUE: WHEN WORK IS PLAY AND PLAY IS LIFE

## Sunday, 10 December

Everyone except David has arrived at Frank's house. Louise came early to help Frank, leaving David to get a meal for the children, and to wait with them until the baby-sitter arrived. By 5:45 they decide to start without David, since they don't want to go on as late as the week before.

HENRY: Frank, are you going to start us off tonight?

FRANK: That's fine with me. I was going to talk about what I think are some interesting new things happening in one of my grade ten math classes, but now that I've gone over Chapter Four I think I can talk about it in terms of what Whitehead says there. When I reread that chapter I realized, if you don't get too bogged down in details, that there is a very strong idea running throughout. As I understand it, Whitehead is emphasizing that an educated person, whatever his or her special interest, skill, vocation, or whatever, would have some kind of a "vision," with the specialty as part of that vision.

GLENDA: Yes, I like this idea of a "vision." I know it's important, and I know that although I haven't called it that to myself, I'm always trying to find one that makes sense to me. I don't like just being occupied with separate tasks in school without some big idea to give them some meaning, to make them seem really worthwhile, to give some sense of where, altogether, they are leading.

LOUISE: Otherwise it's just a rather boring routine, which quickly becomes a drag, right? I felt this when I stopped work to have my children. After the first excitement of seeing them as babies and the continuous work of looking after them, I began to resent going through the same things day after day, you know, cooking, cleaning, shopping, washing. Then a friend loaned me a wonderful book on child care. After reading it I had the clearest sense that everything happening to the children was of tremendous importance to their later lives. Then I began to get a vision of the kind of home atmosphere I wanted to create for them, for the sake of their future, not just their present needs. I started to see all the little demands and chores in the light of this, and they all began to matter in a new way. And my energy and my enjoyment came back.

FRANK: That's how I understand Whitehead on this. The vision gives a special meaning to all the small tasks that they didn't have before. You have a strong idea of something good they could all contribute to, and you do them differently, make changes.

MARIA: You start getting creative, don't you? Thinking of new ways to do things, and what was just work starts to feel more like play, although it's still difficult at times, and it's a serious kind of play. Whitehead says all that in one way or another, and I think he's right, but I also think it can't be any old vision. It has to make real sense to you.

HENRY: And there can be muddled visions and evil visions, can't there?

FRANK: Yes. That's probably why Whitehead uses the ancient Benedictine monks as an example.

JERRY: I didn't like that. I thought he was almost suggesting that we ought to have their kind of Christian vision, and I don't see why we should or even that we can in this day and age.

FRANK: No, you've missed the point, Jerry. He doesn't say anything about having to be religious.

CRAIG: He does at the end of Chapter One.

FRANK: Somehow that's different. I don't think he means that in the sense of having a particular religion. But let's stick to Four for the moment. At the end, page 58, he says this: "I recur to the thought of the Benedictines, who saved for mankind the vanishing civilization of the ancient world by linking together knowledge, labor, and moral energy." And he says, in effect, that "ideal aims" are important, and we needn't be shy of them. The point is, Jerry, the "moral energy" is the thing. Put it together with the required knowledge, and there's your vision. It's not a moralistic vision—where you're harangued about what you haven't done and ought to do. It's a vision of some genuinely good human purpose you can work for. You don't have to be religious in the sense you're thinking of. The Benedictine monks in this chapter stand for the ideal of working together for the common purpose of realizing what matters most for human beings. Think of the monk working in the monastery garden. He didn't just see himself as growing things to eat or heal illness. There was a meaning to it beyond those basic practicalities.

MARIA: This really doesn't sound like you at all, Frank. Are you having a joke on us? You're usually the one who gets sarcastic when you smell anything like a vision around.

FRANK: For your information, Maria, I used to have one. But I guess I've become a bit sour and disillusioned somehow. However, I am capable of change, you know.

MARIA: All right, all right. I only wondered, and you must admit you've certainly fed that idea of yourself.

FRANK: Well, I've found that most of the visions being followed don't seem to stand up to ten minutes of hard scrutiny, and I find it difficult to respect people who clutch onto them for the sake of something, anything, to believe in. However, I can see that Whitehead is nobody's fool, and I can sense some solid ideas coming into view that I want to follow up.

HENRY: On the other hand, I doubt if anyone is completely a fool, and some visions might reveal their value only after several years of scrutiny. Perhaps you prefer to know, rather than believe, Frank, and in that I can sympathize. But before you go any further, or get taken any further, can you pull together in a few words what you think is Whitehead's general meaning of "vision"?

FRANK: As I see it, a vision is some large idea of a way of life, and of a quality of life. And whatever one is doing helps or hinders this in becoming reality. Whitehead's hinting at a very good way of life that can be brought into being by what we are doing as teachers. If our teaching does this, then it's worth being called educating.

LOUISE: That pretty well describes what I got from the chapter so far as the notion of a vision goes. But I'd like to hear what happened in your class. You said it connected with all this.

FRANK: It must have been about two weeks ago that one of the students said something that reminded me of a book that I used to like very much: Edwin Abbott's *Flatland*. Abbott was a nineteenth century mathematics teacher, and he wrote a little story book about what it is like to live in a one, two, three, and perhaps four dimensional world. Anyway, on an impulse I stopped what we were doing and asked the students how many dimensions they thought they lived in. Most said three, but one of them realized nothing could happen, I mean, come about, if that were so, and that there had to be a fourth.

CRAIG: A fourth dimension of space?

FRANK: Yes.

CRAIG: Why is a fourth required? Isn't that just a mathematical idea?

FRANK: Not if the fourth is time.

ANNE: I can see that time is needed for anything to happen, but I don't see that time is a dimension of space.

FRANK: That's exactly the difficulty they—the students—felt. Well, we were still talking about it when the end of the period came, but at the next class, two days later, one student showed me a copy of E. Hinton's *The Fourth Dimension*, which he had found in some library. Another student asked me about a section in a popular physics book on Minkowski's space-time cones—part of the mathematics that turned out to be so useful to Einstein for his general theory of relativity. You see, in both books time is being regarded as in some way a fourth dimension of space. Then, when the class was about to start, another student asked why they couldn't write a story about dimensions in the way Abbott had done. I said they could, and some wanted to start right away and some didn't believe me. So I told them to break up into discussion groups of about four, try to work out what kind of difficulties they would have if they were two-dimensional creatures trying to exist in our world. I said that when they got an idea to start them off they could start writing a story.

MARIA: What happened?

FRANK: Oh, they fooled about a bit, but mostly the discussion got quite serious and heated, and then they were eventually all writing. Before the class ended some read their stories out, and the rest did so at the next class. Some of the stories were extremely clever, I thought, and one of the most interesting came from a girl who usually does very poorly and shows no interest in anything. She even worked out in her mind that if you were two-dimensional and stood up vertically on the surface of the earth, you would fall right through to the center of the earth and be consumed in the heat there. With her two-dimensional society, there was a punishment to fit the crime of making a weapon of war: you were stood upright and down you went and that was the end of you.

GLENDA: Why would a two-dimensional person fall into the center of the earth if upright?

CRAIG: Because if you were two-dimensional, Glenda, you wouldn't have any thickness.

ANNE: The ultimate anorexia! (*David appears in the living room doorway, standing with knitted brows and gaping mouth.*)

DAVID: What on earth are you all talking about? (*They see David in the doorway, realize what nonsense the snippet he heard must have sounded, and break out in laughter.*)

LOUISE: This is just high level mathematical physics, David. You wouldn't understand it. Come on, get a cup of coffee, and I'll tell you what has happened. (*David and Louise disappear whispering into the kitchen, and the discussion starts up again.*)

FRANK: Okay. There's more to this story. Let me tell you the rest. For a start they listened intently as the stories were read, and listening intently in grade ten is not something I often see. They were sometimes quite amazed at each other's ideas, ideas that had never occurred to them. I suspect it hadn't occurred to them, or to me, just how original and thoughtful their fellow students could be. I sensed a kind of new respect for each other in the class. (*Frank pauses, looking into space.*)

MARIA: Yes? What then?

FRANK: What then? Well, then I wondered how on earth I would get them back next class to the normal math curriculum. So I started off as usual, but one student asked if we would continue talking about time and space later on. I said yes, and that was all. The students got on with their work quietly and sensibly, but were more open about difficulties and called on me for help much more readily than usual. Somehow, it was all much friendlier, and I felt I was being respected and really used as a teacher for the first time in a long time. At the end of the class a student stayed behind, with a couple of friends hovering, and said that Mary's story of the fate of two dimensional weapon-makers had made him think of the number three. He said that being of three or higher dimensions could save people from that danger and asked if there is anything special about the number three.

GLENDA: So what did you say?

FRANK: I asked him what he had in mind. He replied that he had been brought up as a Catholic and suddenly wondered why the Trinity was holy. He had also thought about the way two people often get into an argument and can't resolve it, but that a third person can often help them to agree again, or at least feel comfortable with their differences. Then he pointed out the solidity of triangles if you use them in building, and asked again if three isn't some kind of special number. He asked if I thought he was way off, or if there might be something in it.

MARIA: I hope you didn't laugh!

FRANK: I couldn't laugh. I was struck dumb for a moment. I've never heard Bill Schmidt say anything thoughtful, ever. And he was serious, even if a bit shy. But I was also struck by his idea. I said, truthfully, that I really didn't know, but that perhaps there is something special about three, and I would think about it. He was quite satisfied, even relieved, and went off with his friends. Anyway, the next day at the start of class, there he was with his hand up as soon as I put an algebraic formula on the board. He said something like: "x and y and z can stand for any number we want, but do we know what a number is?"

HENRY: What a wonderful question. How did you handle that?

FRANK: I didn't. The class handled it. Some started laughing and said poor old Bill still didn't know what a number is. Someone said with gleeful sarcasm that a number is one or two or three, and so on. The class thought that was a good joke. Bill didn't know what to say, but knew they didn't understand his question. He looked to me to help out, so I asked for anyone in the class to say what made one, two, three, and so on, numbers. (*Frank picks up some notes he has made.*) The replies went something like this:

"They're just words that we've agreed on."

"No they aren't. The words stand for the numbers."

"There are twenty-six desks in the this room. We don't just agree to say 'twenty-six.' We count and find out."

"But we agree to use the word 'twenty-six.'"

"And the French agree to say '*vingt-six.*' So what? It's still the same number, even if the word is different. Numbers must be something else. We could use any word we like, but the number would be the same."

"Very smart. But you still haven't said what a number is."

And so it went round for a while, and I just listened. Gradually they became quiet, and someone said, "Mr. Lederer, I don't think we know what a number is."

So I said, "Well you know something about numbers. You know that two times three equals six and seven plus four equals eleven. You know there are twenty-six and not thirty desks in here." (*Frank looks at his notes again.*) The conversation went on like this:

"Yes, but that's knowing how to do things with numbers. That's not knowing what a number is."

"You just see there are twenty-six desks."

"You do not. You see desks, not numbers."

"Then a number is an idea. It's something in the mind."

"If you can see there are twenty-six desks, the numbers can't just be in your mind. The desks aren't just in your mind are they? If they were, you'd be sitting on the floor!"

"You wouldn't. The floor would be in your mind, too!"

"Perhaps everything is in the mind."

And so it went round again, and when it tailed off, I asked again if they knew what a number is. Some said, "No," and others said "Yes, but we can't define it." Some looked as if they weren't sure whether some trick was being played on them or not. Then one bright young lady got a gleam in her eye, and asked me if I knew what a number is.

MARIA: So what did you say?

FRANK: I said, and I quote: "Frankly, I don't know."

JERRY: Did you get a riot?

FRANK: No, just a few laughs, I'm glad to say. But then they were smiling in disbelief, so I said, truthfully, that I was serious. The same girl got the gleam again and asked if I should be teaching a math class if I don't know what a number is.

MARIA: That was a good move. How did you deal with that?

FRANK: In a way, the bell saved me. So I said, "Well, if you can find the definition of a number, agreed upon by all mathematicians of repute, and show it to me at the next class, I will resign."

JERRY: And did they?

FRANK: Fortunately not.

MARIA: There isn't an agreed definition, I suppose. And you knew that.

FRANK: I knew that I didn't think there was one, but I had some nervous moments over the next few days.

HENRY: Frank, this is a lovely story, but you're telling it for a point, aren't you? What is your point?

FRANK: I do have a point, yes. What do you all think the point is?

MARIA: Is it a true story?

FRANK: Quite true.

DAVID: (*He is sipping his coffee and listening carefully.*) The point could be: you managed to seize the opportunity to launch a romance stage in math learning. They discovered that math can be fascinating, mind-boggling, perhaps for the first time.

ANNE: More than that. The students went further. They actually wanted some precision in their learning. They virtually demanded it.

DAVID: Agreed. But if the learner does enter a romance stage, of course, he or she wants precision, just as we do now about the point of Frank's story, now that he's piqued our curiosity. We want a precise answer, and one that looks like the right answer.

FRANK: Well, what you say is right, I think, but I was after something slightly different. Before, as a math teacher, I was like the "employers" Whitehead talks about in Chapter Four, who expect their workers to do rather meaningless, and so boring, routine tasks, no questions asked. But what has happened is that the students in that class no longer see math as a boring drudgery imposed on them. Their attitude has subtly changed. They seem to see math, judging by their questions and remarks, as rather mysterious, bigger than they realized, governing almost everything they think and do, and yet hiding in the wings. It is as if they suddenly realized for the first time that math points to something really there, in the world, around them and in them, and not just in a school textbook. Yet they can't seem to get a grip on it. It slips out of their fingers. A vision of life inescapably involving numbers at every turn is dawning on them, and with the vision they feel differently about the math they do at school. They are more serious, more questioning, intrigued. And at the same time, I'm not treated as the irritating "boss," but in a more friendly way, as someone who can help them, and will, but also as someone who, like them, is ultimately mystified by mathematics, a sort of fellow traveler. I look forward to school each morning these days, rather then groaning at the sound of the alarm.

CRAIG: In one way, Frank, I like the sound of what's happening in that class, but there's also a curriculum the students have to get through and have to know. If there are too many diversions of the sort you described, how are you going to get through?

HENRY: You're right, Craig, the curriculum has to be worked through and understood, and much of it is important knowledge which does have to be understood, not just because of the exams, but because modern life requires it. Also, mathematics is, or can be, a powerful way to see what it means for thinking to be disciplined and precise. Whitehead explains this use of math in Chapter Four. The problem is, as Whitehead says, and as Frank has found out by experience, when the set curriculum is studied as if it were disconnected from actual life, living persons have difficulty mustering any energy to work with it. It has to be seen as part of some larger meaningful whole, the meaningful whole that life is. And helping the students to see it that way, and feel it that way, is an essential part of "teaching the curriculum." Also, if you do math as if it were disconnected from life, just as routine, pointless exercises, you're presenting math falsely. That means you're not teaching math properly, I mean, in a way that's true to math itself. We wouldn't even have math as a crucial part of our culture if the mathematical pioneers through history had not discovered it to be an unavoidable and intriguing part of life, with immense consequences.

FRANK: What's more, Craig, I've found that once the students do have some vision that math is felt to be part of, they are much more willing to get down to carefully, painstakingly working through examples till they see the principles that are needed.

ANNE: But also, Frank, you couldn't have sparked their interest in math unless at some point you had been fascinated with math yourself.

FRANK: Well, that's true. It started because I began talking about an aspect of math that interests me. As a matter of fact, until that point I had somehow forgotten that math did, and does, interest me.

GLENDA: I liked the part where you talked about the changed relationship between you and the students, and between the students themselves. This has happened to me over and over. When I can get the students to find something that interests them in the work, they feel differently about me, and I feel differently about them. They don't see me as a taskmaster, and I don't see them as a rebellious lot of silly, exhausting kids. We like each other more, we respect each other more. Yes, that's it; we respect each other. They listen to me in a quite different way, and I really start listening to them, taking their questions, the things that interest them, their difficulties, more seriously. I don't think we take the quality of relationship in the classroom and school seriously enough.

ANNE: I agree with that. I don't think we can teach properly—especially in the sense of educating—unless there is the right kind of relationship.

FRANK: I must say though, I did feel uncertain about allowing discussion of fiction, and writing stories, and what is as much physics or cosmology as math, in a math class. I thought: if this gets around, I'll have a few awkward questions to answer from the principal, or other teachers.

HENRY: Don't worry, Frank; you can answer those questions. Remember what Whitehead says about "the principle of the coordination of studies," and "the fatal disconnection of subjects which kills the vitality of our modern curriculum"? Of course, you can't just quote Whitehead. That isn't what I mean. I mean that there are strong arguments in favor of your recent approach, and the elements of those arguments are in Whitehead's book. But you have to be able to argue your approach in your own way, and that requires you first to understand thoroughly the reasons for it yourself. Now, am I the only one who feels like taking a break at this point?

After about a twenty-minute break, Henry suggests they carry on the discussion, and he himself starts it.

HENRY: I think it would be worth talking some more about Whitehead's notion of "vision." We already know that he's not referring to the sort of vision that the Old Testament prophets are reported to have had. Nor does he seem to have in mind any particular religious, social, or political ideology, like Baptist Christianity or Marxism. A problem with talk of a "vision" is that it so easily sounds pretentious or like some unrealistic utopian dream. Acknowledging this, Whitehead shows he's thoroughly aware that "people are shy of ideals," and that up to a point he's sympathetic with them. He's quite clear that any simple-mindedness about this reduces the idea of a vision to absurdity. On page 44, he says: "We are agreed that an employer who conducted his workshop on the principle that 'work should be play' would be ruined in a week."

Nonetheless, the vision he argues for, in a subtle and knowledgeable way, is that work can be play, in the sense of being enjoyable and adequately meaningful. His basic reasons for this are, first, that life thereby takes on a precious quality, and second, that there is no necessity for it to be otherwise. Then he sets about showing how simply school education can take on this quality, and indirectly can show students how later to infuse their own and others' lives with this same quality.

So "play" has a special meaning here. It's not "playing around." It's more what math started to become when Frank's students got the first glimmerings of the real interest and importance of math in virtually every kind of event making up daily life.

JERRY: On pages 43 and 44, Whitehead quotes Bernard Shaw to express what his own ideal is: "It is a commonwealth in which work is play, and play is life." If we take "play" in the sense you've indicated, is there much difference between this vision of his and the one we examined before, where education is thought of as a special guidance in the understanding of life as an art?

HENRY: At root, probably not. But until one hears the details of what these highly general statements mean to the writer, they are suspect of being breezy but empty high-mindedness. And Whitehead has all kinds of different details under each heading, and those details matter to our decision to take him seriously or not. When you look at the details of what is said in each chapter, you can see that he is not repeating himself, but adding crucial detail to the meaning of the ideals he is suggesting.

ANNE: Also, I find the difference in the wording of the ideal or vision helpful in getting a more rounded understanding of it. In Chapter Three where he mentions education and the comprehension of the art of life, he emphasizes that human beings are not mechanisms and that as organisms the main impetus for the sort of people they become and the sort of life they lead comes from within. We see that this implies the necessity for the energy of interest and for the right direction of learning, of understanding. Then the right kind of interest and of understanding requires teachers to respect the romance-precision-generalization schema. Now in Chapter Four Whitehead is emphasizing not the best kind of learning and teaching, though that's there, too. His emphasis is the way the breadth of understanding which encloses the special techniques acquired by individuals makes all the difference to the meaningfulness and enjoyment of those techniques, the effort put in, the quality of work produced. Well, they're all related.

HENRY: They are, yes, but you missed out creativity. There must be room for and encouragement of a creative, innovative use of talent. This is essential to his notion of work felt as play. "In creation only is there vivid insight," Whitehead says. I have it highlighted. Yes, page 53. That's a bold statement, and of great educational importance, if true.

ANNE: All right, yes, creativity does need to be named here. Because, yes, look, when Whitehead talks of breadth of mind, he doesn't mean a big accumulation of disconnected facts in the memory. For him, increasing the breadth of understanding is not a continual·adding on of bits and pieces; it's the result of a creative leap of mind and activity into the student's unknown.

LOUISE: What? If your understanding becomes broader, you know more. That's additive—an addition of more knowledge. I don't understand what you're getting at.

ANNE: There is an increase in knowledge, yes. The trouble is that when people say "increase in knowledge" they're referring to the collection of bits of information in all sorts of fields, the kind of thing TV panel games test the remembrance of. So you can get someone who remembers the titles of pieces of music, the dates of kings and queens, the scores of football matches thirty years ago, and so on, and everyone seems to think this person brilliant for her "breadth" of knowledge. Yet she may hardly have given a thought to understanding life as a whole. The kind of breadth I think really matters, and what Whitehead implies, is where the understanding of one thing leads to the understanding of another, and so on outwards. Like the wave spreading out from a pebble dropped in water. It's all one, not a heap of bits and pieces. That's it! Spreading out, not piling up.

JERRY: If I understand you, I get an image of this process which is helpful to me. In my mind I see a painter brushing in one blade of grass in the middle of his canvas. Then he decides to put in more grass, some flowers, then trees, distant mountains, a cloudy sky, and eventually a whole landscape. Each item led to and connected with every other, and the final painting is the connection of them all in a meaningful whole which the painter himself may have had no clear idea of to start with.

ANNE: That's it. He has added more and more, but what is important to the result—a fine painting, rather than a colorful mess—is the connection of each part to every other part.

HENRY: Yes, I like that painting analogy, but we're going to need an example of this broadening process to ground the meaning that we're after. Especially if we want to translate the idea into practice.

DAVID: What you are all describing as "breadth" of understanding sounds to me like the natural way the mind works, and one of the best places to see this is in children before they've gone to school. Think of any young child; his understanding begins with the recognition of his own feelings and needs, and how these are related to the mother. Gradually he sees some relationship between himself, his mother, and others in the family, and learns to discern who is and who is not in the family. At the same time, beginning with the discernment of the details of one or two rooms in which most of his first few months of life are spent, he sees that these are connected to the other rooms, the house, the garden, and the big "outside" in general. The bedroom is connected with sleep—or his cradle; the kitchen with food; the living room carpet and the grass with the free movement of play, and then with others like himself as playmates. All this obviously develops in his mind in such a way that each new item recognized is seen in its relation to what he already knows something about. It spreads out. It doesn't just add up.

HENRY: All right, yes, let's go on with this some more. Every new item is noticed because it's felt in some way to be connected with his real interests and needs: sleep, love, food, play, security, adventure, playmates, and so on. So interests and needs, and some fair success in getting these satisfied, seem to be essential to this natural broadening out of understanding and knowledge, wouldn't you agree?

DAVID: Yes.

MARIA: What I've just been thinking of is the contrast between my experience of young children learning and many adults I've met, including some university teachers, if you don't mind, Henry.

HENRY: I think I can handle it. What's your idea?

MARIA: That often with adults, if you mention something connected with their field of interest, but they haven't yet put it in that field, they don't want to know. I remember recently when I was at a conference on the psychology of child development, a cognitive psychologist had been talking about Piaget's work on children's logical thinking. I asked a question about something I had read on the contribution of Jungian psychology to our understanding of the literature children benefit most from in the development of their understanding. And he just brushed the question aside with: "Oh, that's depth psychology; that's not my area. I don't touch that."

GLENDA: Is there any reason why he should?

MARIA: Yes. If he's interested in children's thinking and understanding, why wouldn't he let his own understanding spread out into the possibility that the Jungians may have some good ideas on this? My impression is that when their work is taken into consideration, the light that Piaget sheds is a much weaker light than many psychologists and teachers realize. For example, there's evidence that fairy tales, myths, Biblical and Homeric epics and the like are of greater importance to learning in the intuitive-feeling mode of childhood than the kind of Piagetian tasks educators create to stimulate the natural logical development of conceptual thinking. Others argue that abstract thinking is usually demanded at much too early an age, interfering with the way children naturally feel their way into understanding.

DAVID: That accords with Whitehead's conviction that childhood should, overall, be recognized as the first great stage of romance in learning.

MARIA: Because that is the stage of learning where one enters into the beginnings of understanding of something and the mind's grasp on it is vague . but with strong feeling?

DAVID: Yes, and exploring with imagination, intuition and action are much more at the forefront in childhood than precise abstract expression. It's common knowledge that most children find it more satisfying and more appropriate to their mode of understanding things—at least up to about adolescence—to explore and express things with art, drama, story, rather than with highly abstract words in literal prose, or with numbers. All that is just a detailed way of saying that this period of childhood is a natural period in which the romance stage of learning is the most predominant one.

HENRY: All right, I think your example from childhood is a fair one, but what about one from adult experience that we can immediately relate to?

FRANK: Well, I think what I said about the students in my class could be developed a bit to illustrate what Anne is after. As I said, the concept of a dimension came up, and I realized the students were using it very loosely, as in everyday speech. That's when I thought of *Flatland* and mentioned it as a way of getting them to think more about the concept. So from some simple calculation of the dimensions of a room in a house, we moved to consider dimensions of space and time: how many we think there are or may be; whether time is another dimension of space; how all this affects the way we understand our lives with space and time relations in everything. That led to the question of the nature of number and the question of mind, conceptuality, and how concepts relate to the experienced world.

CRAIG: And don't forget the student who began to get into the rather esoteric questions about the number three. That was beginning to get into some kind of mysticism.

HENRY: Well, we're looking at the way understanding connects idea to idea and idea to experience, moving outwards, so to speak. In that way you could easily see the interested intelligence feeling its way into philosophy, relativity physics, and, as you say, Craig, into mysticism or religion in some very general sense. After all, the great mystics seem to overlap with modern physicists in the discovery of timelessness—the other side of time as we normally think of it. While one person might go in this direction, another might feel moved to explore the unreality of time in the sense of the irrelevance of clock time to subjective time.

LOUISE: Subjective time? Do you mean the way children, when told it's time for bed, often protest because at the time they don't feel like sleeping?

HENRY: That's exactly what I mean. Or take the frequent occurrence of frustration for teachers and students when the buzzer indicates a change of class just as they are getting involved in some project and don't want to stop. Organized, clock time says, "Time to stop," but subjective time says, "Time to continue."

FRANK: Or they come to a natural stop before the buzzer goes off, but are forced to carry on. That's what I think Whitehead is suggesting in this chapter when he talks of the need for regular refreshment. Students are often expected to go too long in one kind of activity, and we should be sensitive to the need to refresh the mind with a change. If the work was precise calculation, the change to art or craft work would be appropriate—where the mind can roam more freely and creatively, free of rules and abstractions.

HENRY: Yes, that's what he has in mind. Are we all fairly clear, then, on what Anne was talking about in the distinction between "breadth of knowledge" as an accumulation of discrete bits and pieces of information, and "breadth of knowledge" as the moving of the intelligence outward in a wider sweep, as the connection of one thing or idea with another becomes apparent?

FRANK: And that for one's specialist activity to be alive with enough meaning it must be seen in the context of this wider sweep of understanding?

HENRY: Alive, yes, but also if this wider sweep does not continue, the activity is artificially specialist, since inquiry is not being allowed to move wherever relevant connections exist.

JERRY: (*Who is fidgeting with some dissatisfaction and chooses this pause to voice it*) We skated over the topic of art, as it comes up in this chapter, far too quickly. I think we need to go back to it. For Whitehead, art is not only for refreshment, but for the release of creative energy. Or perhaps I should say, the best refreshment is the kind of creative energy released in an especially effective way by artistic involvement. Before, I hadn't thought too much about artistic activity in general, though I was well aware, in my own way, of this refreshment by the creativity of art in music. And it isn't only the energy of creativity, the importance of art is that it gives beauty as well as creativity. Beauty is wonderfully refreshing. I like to see the students' faces when they've practiced a choral piece to high perfection; then, they sing it all through and stop, quite stunned by the beauty of what they've produced. I can imagine that happening with the appreciation of literature and creative writing, too. Though I don't really see why Whitehead keeps talking of literature and art separately. I suppose it could be because in school and university literature is treated too much as if it were like a machine to be taken apart into all its little pieces, and then you are left with a heap of bits instead of a work of art, an illuminating whole.

HENRY: I don't know why Whitehead talks of art and literature as if they were separate, but I like your idea—that would seem valid in any case.

FRANK: It just occurred to me that this "refreshment" of creative art was exactly what happened in my math class when the students began writing stories. I can see Whitehead's point only too well about the muddled assumption that students focusing on technical skills in some area like metal work don't need art—including literature. For a start, I would encourage them to create metal sculptures with their new skills in welding.

DAVID: We also missed the part, on page 58, where Whitehead says art and literature give vision. I imagine from what you said, Frank, that for you the importance of that book—*Flatland,* is it?—was that it gave you some kind of new vision. (*Frank nods agreement.*) And when someone creates a serious work of art they seem to have some kind of a vision, however vague, behind the endeavor. The artist is not just playing about with pretty shapes and colors; he's trying to convey what he feels is some important meaning or truth. I would think that can be as true of the child creating art as it is of Picasso. So art does stimulate that larger sweep of meaning which we're calling "vision."

JERRY: But it must be real art. When I see twenty-five identical pictures or stories in a classroom I know there's no real art going on there.

MARIA: I've been thinking for a while about subjective time, and art . . . and also mysticism. There's some connection, isn't there? Let me see if I can pull it together. I've remembered that when I occasionally paint, I usually become so lost in what I'm doing that I lose all sense of time. Well, not exactly all sense of time; I mean the feeling of time passing. It's as if I'm simply all the time in the present. Then I'll perhaps notice the clock and be amazed that what I would have judged as about an hour is four hours on the clock. And— now I know this sounds ridiculous—what seemed like maybe an hour at most also felt, while I was actually painting, like days and days. Even that's not quite right, because I only have that notion if I suddenly think of time, but when I'm lost in the painting and not really thinking, there doesn't seem to be time at all—just always what is happening, present-ly.

HENRY: There doesn't seem to be time at all, you say? I suppose you mean no sense of time passing—you know, from past to present to the future?

MARIA: Yes, exactly. Perhaps that's something like a mystical conscious-ness. I don't know, but it's very peaceful—there's no anxiety about getting on to this or that by such-and-such a time. But what I was also thinking of was Whitehead's frequent talk of the "present" in Chapter One. I wanted to talk about that weeks ago, but it got lost in other things. There is that strange pas-sage, at the end of Chapter One, where Whitehead says . . . let me find it . . . yes, he says: "And the foundation of reverence is this perception, that the pre-sent holds within itself the complete sum of existence, backwards and forwards, that whole amplitude of time, which is eternity."

ANNE: Well, he also says something like that on page 3. Look: "The present contains all that there is. It is holy ground, for it is the past, and it is the fu-ture."

MARIA: All right, then, look just before that: "No more deadly harm can be done to young minds than by the depreciation of the present." This is my query, you see, Anne; just what is Whitehead trying to get across in all this talk of the "present"?

HENRY: I've got an idea. Let's try to understand it this way, Maria. Where is the past?

MARIA: Nowhere. It isn't.

HENRY: You mean, it doesn't exist?

MARIA: Yes.

HENRY: What we discussed five minutes ago doesn't now exist?

MARIA: No. It existed five minutes ago.

HENRY: What did we discuss five minutes ago?

MARIA: Oh, I don't know. Art and the refreshment of art, probably.

HENRY: How do you know that?

MARIA: I remember it, of course.

HENRY: So does that past event have no kind of existence at all in the present, now?

MARIA: Do you mean it exists now in our memories?

HENRY: Well, does it?

MARIA: No, I mean, sort of. If I remember, it is re-created, but not exactly. A copy comes into existence. But not the original.

HENRY: I agree with that. Would you say that a past event has some kind of existence in the present?

MARIA: Yes, I think so.

HENRY: And could our present moment of discussion exist without that past event?

MARIA: No. What we are now discussing led on from that past discussion.

HENRY: Could we say then that the past event lives on in the present event because it gives some of the shape, the character, of what is happening now?

MARIA: Some of the shape of the present, yes, but only some, because we might have gone in a different direction, and then the present would be different.

HENRY: Although still bearing something of the character of the past discussion?

MARIA: Yes.

HENRY: Can we say then that the present is always partly shaped by the past?

MARIA: Always? Well, yes, I think we probably can.

HENRY: If instead of discussing art and refreshment in that past, one of us had instead exploded a bomb, the present now would be very different, wouldn't it, very ugly?

MARIA: What a dreadful idea, Henry. Why do you ask that?

HENRY: Because I'm thinking that what we bring about in any "now" will affect what comes about as the new "now."

LOUISE: So that what we do in the present—any present—will affect what can come about in the future?

HENRY: Yes. Whatever one does in the present limits, and to some extent makes possible, what can come about in the future. Even if we now lay the foundation for something really good in the future—and I hope we are—it's still true that our "now" places limits on the shape of the future. They could be desirable or undesirable limits. Maria, where is the future?

MARIA: In the future! Nowhere yet . . . wait! That's a trap, I know. You'll ask me if the future has no existence at all now. Well, if the future at least partly comes out of the present, then in some sense I would have to say that the future already exists in the present.

HENRY: Yes, for example, what we say together now affects what we shall be saying in two minutes.

CRAIG: I can see where you're going, Henry, alias Socrates. If some ground is "holy," something special can happen there. But holy ground can also be desecrated, and that would be said to bring bad luck, or worse. So if you have reverence for the present as "holy ground," you have that reverence because you realize that what happens now must affect, well or badly, what happens in the future. We often say, "Oh, what an awful time this is; how did it come about like this?" So we obviously recognize that what happened in the past affects what happens in the present. But if we're not serious we pretend it's "bad luck" or all the fault of others, that our past was somehow beyond our control. If we're serious, we look very carefully at the past to see what we ourselves did wrong, so that we have a good chance of not repeating those mistakes again. I don't mean that we condemn ourselves. I mean we look back to see what we can change. So we have a responsibility for making the present the kind of present that the best kind of future can come out of.

HENRY: You make my point exactly, Craig.

FRANK: And presumably this has something to do with education?

GLENDA: Frank, can't you see? If you continually make the present dull, boring, frustrating, for the student, you would, for example, give her a future in which she resents learning, or can't do any more significant learning.

HENRY: True, but don't forget you would be in that present also. Your future would also be affected by the quality of that present. I wish teachers would also think of themselves and how they are affecting themselves in the future by what they create in school in the present. Teacher burn-out doesn't just happen by external circumstances; it happens very much as a result of the way teachers are working, relating, in each present moment. And teachers can change that, change themselves. Then the external situation will also change somewhat.

LOUISE: Wouldn't it also follow that with this idea, we could be more tolerant of the students' negative attitudes and habits? After all, what they are now is very much determined by what kind of a past they've been subjected to.

MARIA: Yes, I've noticed that you have a tendency to push all the responsibility onto the students, Frank, as if they are in complete control of their attitudes. You know, you say, "Oh, the students are dull, unwilling," and so on. That sounds as if you're unsympathetic to the fact that they are themselves badly affected by the examples of parents, people they see on TV, other teachers, other students, friends, other classes. But when you recently stopped blaming others, and changed what you were doing, they also changed and showed you a new side of themselves.

LOUISE: Fair enough, Marie, but why pick on Frank? We can all catch ourselves doing this often. You may even be doing it in taking Frank as your example rather than yourself. That's almost like saying it's always someone else and not yourself, isn't it?

MARIA: Lou, have you really been listening to Frank? Why, up until tonight . . . .

HENRY: Maria, are you really listening to Lou? What she suggests is not absurd. There might be something in it. There's no need to defend yourself. Why not just think awhile about what she's said? (*pause*) I'd like to go back a moment to the issue of teachers giving themselves consideration. What you said is surely right, Lou, that you can find more sympathy for the students if you are aware that they are affected by situations in their pasts. This could be as immediate as what just happened in the hallway before class, or as continuous as the effect of a family that doesn't value education. But you rushed us past this point about the well-being of teachers. Can we dwell on this some more? How do all of you see this?

DAVID: Well, at first I thought you were suggesting that teachers just "look after number one," as they say. But now I think you're saying that teachers need, if they are to be in top form and liking their work, to create an atmosphere in their classes that refreshes or renews them as well as the students. Otherwise, the teachers will be of little use to the students.

HENRY: Yes, refresh themselves, that's it. Look at it this way, "re-fresh," with a hyphen. Successful teaching, that is, educating, needs teachers who feel fresh, alive, energetic, creative. Since teachers spend so much time in the classroom, I think they need to ask if the atmosphere of that class exhausts and discourages, or whether it interests, amuses, revitalizes themselves. Psychologically, it's analogous to being sensible enough to nurture your body with food, drink, rest, and so on. And if the students are bored and frustrated, that helps create an atmosphere which exhausts the teacher. I don't just mean it makes the teacher tired; I mean it exhausts and discourages. If, as teachers, you, we, encourage the students with interest and vitality, that will create an atmosphere which revitalizes us, right in the midst of hard work.

ANNE: You mean that then we may, will, get physically and mentally tired, but not depressed in spirit?

HENRY: Exactly.

DAVID: So if we create an atmosphere in which the students are interested and engaged, where the learning has a lot of personally felt significance, we don't get the exhaustion of discouragement and the bad relations which follow that?

HENRY: Yes, and it's my experience that physical and mental tiredness are easily overcome with sleep, exercise, doing something different with the mind, eating intelligently, having the right kind of friends, and so on. But exhaustion of the spirit seems to be the very opposite of the energy of a strong vision, and in the long run far more draining to the person, and far harder to reverse. Look here . . . on page 41 Whitehead warns us of the danger of this: "I have no doubt that unless we can meet the new age with new methods, to sustain for our populations the life of the spirit, sooner or later, amid some savage outbreak of defeated longings, the fate of Russia will be the fate of England."

DAVID: You know, I think I've hit on something important. We've said that personally appreciated learning—in other words, the right sort of learning—keeps the student fresh and alive in mind.

ANNE: If it's really educating you're about.

DAVID: Yes. That is exactly what I mean. Now this is my idea: why shouldn't the same be true of the teacher? I mean, if the teachers, while teaching, are learning something that feels of significance to them, that kind of learning will also revitalize them. Doesn't that make a nice kind of sense? Look at it. If the teachers teach so as to learn things that feel worthwhile to themselves, then they have a built-in revitalization system in their work. Or put it this way—I like this: the better the teachers' learning, while they teach, the better the students' learning will be.

HENRY: I like the way you put that, David, because it's so often assumed that the teacher is there only to teach, not to learn. And that's not only naive; it's arrogant.

GLENDA: This is going too fast for me. How do we teach so that at the same time we do learning that excites and renews us? Oh, wait. I can see that we could be watching and learning helpful things about the students.

HENRY: Is that what you had in mind, David?

DAVID: No, but I think it's a good point. What I was thinking of I'm not sure I can talk about clearly—it's a big, vague intuition at the moment. Let me see. It's about the teacher learning something more of the subject itself, or about something that matters to him concerning life in general. I don't know. I can't take it any further.

HENRY: I have a feeling you do know, but as we said with "romance," new understanding begins in vague intuitions. Try this. In his essay, "Harvard: The Future," I remember Whitehead says that for anything we know, we know part of it clearly, part of it vaguely, and there is much more all round it that we don't seem to be at all aware of. Take Frank's case. He, like his students, knows clearly that two times three equals six, vaguely that two or three or six or any number is something not to be perceived by the senses but grasped by the mind. But then his understanding stops completely in front of questions like: "What is it about our universe such that we can't perceive numbers with our senses, and yet they are unavoidably involved somehow in what is captured by sense-perception, so that, for example, we can know that there are twenty-six desks, and not thirty-six?" Is that right, Frank?

FRANK: I couldn't have put it as well myself.

HENRY: All right, now do you remember that in Chapter Three of *The Aims*, Whitehead says that a teacher should be who he really is, an ignorant man thinking, or words to that effect? Well, if for anything we know clearly, and want to teach, we only stick to the part that's already clear to us, we don't learn anything. But what if we also convey to the students what puzzles us, what we aren't sure about? Then we get into an inquiry with the students that virtually forces us to begin to get some clearer understanding of the vague part of our knowledge. So, for Frank, as well as making sure the students know that two times three equals six, he also conveys the fact that he doesn't know what a number is, but would like to.

JERRY: Wouldn't he have to feel secure enough to be able, as a teacher, to admit ignorance?

HENRY: Certainly. But we need to stop projecting the absurd image of ourselves, teachers, as those who know all that needs to be known, as infallible knowledge-transmitting machines. Surely a teacher who educates sees teaching primarily as engaging students in inquiry into important matters. When you see educating in that way, you no longer hesitate to talk openly about what you don't understand. I would call this "working on the boundaries of our ignorance," that is, in the murky and alluring area between what one knows clearly and what one doesn't know at all. Whitehead has a provocative discussion of this area he calls "penumbral darkness" in his essay "Harvard: The Future."

DAVID: I've got that. It's in A.H. Johnson's *Whitehead's American Essays in Social Philosophy*. About the way confusion over the idea of knowing ruins educational practice. Isn't that it?

HENRY: Yes. So working on the boundary of ignorance makes sense for learning, doesn't it? If you're really learning, you're coming to understand what you don't already know, not what you already know clearly. It follows that for educational learning, both the student and the teacher need to be pushing into their areas of ignorance, not cowering timidly in the shelter of the few things they have quite clear. Frank, for example, admitted to the students in his math class that he doesn't know what a number is. Inquiry is what matters, not adding up smugly what one already knows.

If teachers keep themselves limited to what they already know clearly, and just try to transmit that, they're bound to get bored and dispirited. David's little Socratic interlude with Glenda was a nice example of one way to avoid that trap. He used what he knows to frame questions which moved Glenda from what she knows into seeing for herself what she barely knows and what she doesn't know at all. And it was very alive for him also, because finding the right sequence of questions challenged him to be creative with what he knows, in a way that put him at risk. At any point he could have made a mistake or discovered some error in his thinking.

GLENDA: That gives me another idea. I can see that if I ask questions from what I know to what I don't know, I'm entering into what for me is a mystery. And one thing I do know is that children love a mystery; it really excites them and draws them in.

HENRY: And adults, or anyone. I'm sure we all learn most when we move into what's mysterious to us, rather than hiding in the illusory security of the known.

DAVID: So if as a teacher you convey what is mysterious to you, you awaken. the sense of the mysterious in the students?

HENRY: Yes, and that surely is what happened in Frank's class, isn't it?

LOUISE: I'm afraid I don't think I can stay awake much longer. Shall we stop soon? (*Several voices, and yawns, agree, and everyone starts pulling together books and papers.*)

DAVID: Hold on a minute. I suppose we aren't going to be meeting for a while, what with Christmas and starting the new term. Shouldn't we plan something for the future?

HENRY: I've just remembered something I meant to discuss with you. A colleague of mine has been experimenting with a new approach that seems very useful to her students. I think you might like to use it to keep these ideas alive in your minds till we next meet. It could also be a way for each of you to have a period of digesting them. Her students keep personal journals of their own thoughts, and regularly share them with each other. They comment in each other's journals—they are dialogue-journals. Couldn't we split into pairs, try that for a while, and then later decide when to meet as a group again?

JERRY: I can see David is enthusiastic, and it sounds worth trying. Let's do it. (*Most are nodding agreement, and some seem unsure.*)

HENRY: Well, obviously no one has to do it, but if it turned out to be good for you, it might well be something new to try in your own classrooms. All right, you all look fairly willing now, so there's the question of what pairs. My suggestion is that rather different personalities could give the best results.

A quite heated discussion begins around who will pair with whom, and for a moment everyone seems to be talking at once. Gradually some agreement is reached, and the pairing that emerges is Glenda with Frank, Maria with Anne, Louise with Jerry, and David with Craig. The pairs start moving off to make their own arrangements with each other, and then begin leaving. Finally, after a lot of "Happy Christmas" calls from the doorway, Frank, Louise, and David are left and begin cleaning up.

# PART 3

## The Journal Dialogues

# Eight

# FIRST EXCHANGE OF JOURNALS: GLENDA AND FRANK

## 1. Glenda Martin's Journal

### 11 December

I've never kept a journal before, let alone given it to someone else to read and respond to, so I'll start now while the dialogues are still fresh in my mind. Otherwise, I have a feeling I'll procrastinate nervously and not start at all. Should I be writing these thoughts in the journal at all? Aren't they just personal stuff, not about ideas? Yes, and no. Now I come to think of it, my anxiety must come from something. What? Right—an idea! Which idea? Let's see. This is strange; I don't know how I could "see" that, and yet I have a sense of it emerging. Anxious about what? That's it—anxious because I have an idea that I won't be good at this. So there is another idea—that I should do something well or not at all. How idiotic that idea is, when it's flushed out and displayed in the light of day. If this journal is worth doing, what does it matter about good and bad? Whose standards anyway? Well, I also have an idea for a new saying: anything worth doing is worth doing badly! What's the alternative? To do something well that isn't worth doing?

That little bit of self-inquiry helped. I don't feel anxious any more. It was interesting how that happened. I only found out what was causing my anxiety when I saw it as a problem, as a puzzle to be solved, and I was able to clarify it as a question to myself. Then the answer emerged gradually, vague at first, but I sensed it coming, and knew what was going to be the answer. That's a romance stage of learning again. Once you have had this pattern of understanding pointed out, you start seeing it all over the place. I wonder why it wasn't obvious before reading Whitehead. I suppose that might be the brilliance of a great mind, to recognize the significance of the obvious and name it so that it doesn't slide away round the edges of conscious awareness. I wonder if the extraordinary is the ordinary seen in its real importance?

I've been thumbing through Whitehead again, and I see he has much to say to me on writing and thinking freely and how I could get stuck thinking that an idea must be good or right. I'm looking at page 47 of *The Aims*, where he says that "education must pass beyond the passive reception of the ideas of others. Powers of initiative must be strengthened." So I go beyond

my passively received idea that what I write must be good and use my own
judgment on what I am capable of doing.

He also thinks that the idea or image of extraordinary people conjured up
in well-selected reading can have a very positive effect on what we think we
are capable of. On page 69, where he talks about the educational possibilities
of literature from various cultures, he emphasizes that simply using such
literature to learn another language is to miss the main educational point.
What is the point?

> The merit of this study in the education of youth is its concreteness, its
> inspiration to action, and the uniform greatness of persons. . . . Their
> aims were great, their virtues were great, and their vices were great. . . .
> Moral education is impossible apart from the habitual vision of
> greatness.

I know that is how I feel about the little I've studied of Socrates in Plato's
dialogues, though I'm not sure exactly what it is about Socrates that attracts
me. I must think this out. Certainly it's his power of thinking things through
clearly, and his confidence in himself around that. But also something about
the way he uses dialogue for it. I don't know. Can't think it out now. Too
tired. Anyway, I've just remembered this a dialogue journal. Why should I do
all the work? I'll pass it on to Frank and see if he can conjure up something
inspiring.

## 2. Frank Lederer's Journal

### 16 December

You didn't waste any time launching your journal, Glenda. The last thing I
ever expected to do on a Saturday is write in a journal, but here goes!

I don't know about inspiring, but I do have thoughts along the lines of
yours. I picked up David's book by Theodore Roszak, *The Cult of
Information*, by mistake, and now I can't put it down. It's made me do a lot of
re-thinking of my use of computers in school. What I'm looking at in chapter
ten has much to do with using stories and dialogue in educating. One thing at
a time.

You talked about Whitehead's suggestion that literature, great stories
about great people, has much more value in the curriculum than merely learning a language (or some history, for that matter). Roszak has interesting
things to say about this. He thinks education at all levels should deal with big
ideas, what he calls "master ideas," not just little routines in the subject areas.
He reminded me of what happened when I introduced my students to Abbott's
story, *Flatland*. Roszak's idea is that the master ideas, the ones that have had

powerful effects, good and bad, on everything in history, should be studied for that very reason. Well, not exactly studied, not by children. Instead, the master ideas should be lived with in the stories of the lives of real and imaginary people who lived out of big ideas. Listen to Roszak (page 215) on this. Doesn't it sound similar to Whitehead's idea? "Every healthy culture puts its children through such a Homeric interlude when epic images, fairy tales, *chansons de geste*, Bible stories, fables, and legends summon the mind to growing purpose. That interlude lays the foundations of thought." He argues that master ideas are too much in the hands of television and movie opportunists who present at best "a few tawdry images of heroism and villainy," so we need to get back to the undistorted stories themselves. This is not to be done in a heavy way:

> Though the children's grasp of such literature may be simple and playful, they are in touch with material of high seriousness. From the heroic examples before them, they learn that growing up means making projects with full responsibility for one's choices. In short, taking charge of one's life in the presence of a noble standard.

Doesn't that sound like Whitehead's sense of what lays the proper foundation for a "moral education?"

On page 216, Roszak also has something to say about Socratic dialogue in adolescence, and this might be what your reading of Socrates is leading you to. Roszak points out the obvious, that the characters of such stories are often confused and villainous, and at some point what is really good and what is gloriously villainous in these characters needs to be sorted out: "Homer offers towering examples of courage. Ah, but what is true courage? Socrates asks, offering other, conflicting images, some of which defy Homer. At once, idea is pitted against idea, and the students must make up their own minds, judge and choose." "Make up their own minds," he says. Like that sentence you took from Whitehead: "Powers of initiative must be strengthened." But Roszak points to dialogue, and I wonder why Whitehead doesn't see the value of dialogue, or doesn't talk about it. Roszak says: "Still, no educational theory that lacks such a Socratic counterpoint can hope to free the young to think new thoughts, to become new people, and so to renew the culture." He rounds it all out (for me) on page 219, with this:

> There is a crucial early interval in the growth of young minds when they need the nourishment of value-bearing images and ideas, the sort of Homeric themes that open the adventure of life for them. . . . But once young minds have missed the fairy tales, the epic stories, the myths and legends, it is difficult to go back and recapture them with that fertile sense of naive wonder that belongs to childhood. Similarly, if the taste for Socratic inquiry is not enlivened somewhere in the adolescent years,

the growing mind may form habits of acquiescence that make it difficult to get out from under the dead hand of parental dominance and social authority.

So there we are, Glenda, what do you think? Has all this inspired you? Are you going to launch in with a Homeric interlude for your grade fours, and shatter the clockwork regularity of "following the curriculum?" I hope so. Though I have no suggestions as to what you will say to the parents and your superiors!

Seriously, this concern about dialogue in education is really beginning to interest me. Our dialogues as a group, and those that started up in my math class, were pretty intriguing and useful, and Roszak is persuasive. But the question that remains for me is why dialogue has to be left for the adolescent years. Why not start it earlier? I don't know much about young children, but you may have some ideas. Maria showed me a book called *Dialogues with Children* (by Gareth Matthews, I think), and the bits I skimmed through— actual transcripts of dialogues with children—made it look as if children are good at dialogue, like it, and learn a lot through it. It isn't just discussion— well, that's another issue. Enough for now. My journal enthusiasm has temporarily run out.

# Nine

# SECOND EXCHANGE OF JOURNALS: JERRY AND LOUISE

## 1. Jerry Lovett's Journal

### 16 December

At the moment I have to admit that I don't like trying to write in this journal. If I didn't have an agreement with Louise to exchange journals, I'm quite sure I wouldn't do it. I get an idea, and then when I go to write about it, I feel as if what I say will be wrong or stupid or beside the point. What point? That's interesting. I've just realized in a new way that this is my journal, so that whatever I want to say is to the point! I think I know what is going on here. In school and university what I had to write was being criticized all the time— the thinking, the expression, grammar and spelling, and so on. And the topics were always chosen in detail by the teacher, for everyone, and for no one in particular. The writing wasn't about what was of immediate interest to me. Or it had to be written in a format that felt awkward and alien to me. Except the course with Dr. Green during my B.Ed. work. Right there I had a moment of anxiety as I realized that last statement was a "sentence fragment!" That's the kind of thing that stops me and makes me forget what I was saying. Here I can hardly resist putting the paper away and sitting down to play the piano. Where was I? Dr. Green. She was different. She kept encouraging us to write on issues that we felt concerned about, and to use the books and other materials to help that. I used to get paralyzed at the thought of putting down on paper, to be evaluated, what I really thought. When I finally got my assignment in to her she was very sympathetic to my ideas, but I never got over the nervousness, and she has passed into the "pleasant and curious oddities" section of my memory.

This is a new paragraph mainly because I seem to have gone on too long in the first one, but if it's my journal, what does it matter? I have also had a new idea—please note, ghost-like teachers of English in my mind! I'm supposed to be writing on Whitehead's ideas, but so far all I have done is prattle on about my writing paranoia. Whitehead raised a hundred questions for me, so` where are they now? They seem to have taken to their heels in fright. All right, let's approach this calmly and methodically. I could comment on that interesting chapter on classics in education. Or I could go back to some of those jottings I made during the discussions. I think I'll go back to the notes.

I'm sure there were lots of things I put down that I wanted to follow up. Back to the notes! Come to think of it, if they were musical notes, there would be no problem. Write them or strike them, and I could easily follow with another and another, confident that I would see a way to go with a result worth hearing. I wonder if real writers feel about words the way I feel about musical notes. Suddenly I feel as if I might be beginning to understand how they get started and how they manage to go on and on. Perhaps if I could think of my writing more as a musical composition it would come more easily.

Going through my notes I've stopped dead at a question I put down ages ago, and couldn't find a place in the discussions to bring up. On page 40, Whitehead says: "You cannot, without loss, ignore in the life of the spirit so great a factor as art." Then he goes on to connect "aesthetic emotions" with "vivid apprehensions" and "development of the whole personality." There is something here I want to understand, but it's all moving too fast for me. Life of the spirit? I'm sure that Whitehead sees all this as connected to educating, not to religion as we normally encounter it—churches, theology, worship of God, etc. Even when he criticizes teaching of religion on page 39—that it is a marvel that the religious spirit has survived the "ordeal of religious education"—it seems that his point is really that it hasn't been educating. I suppose he means that it has been a dull imposition of inert ideas about religion. That's about the most literal sense of "soul murder" that I could think of! But I wish he would say, in the light of the rest of his discussion, religious teaching, not "religious education." After all, he has, in effect, argued throughout that teaching as such is not necessarily educational in the really serious sense of that word.

So I'm stuck at the question of why "aesthetic emotions" are supposed to be so crucial to the "life of the spirit." I've never thought of my students' aesthetic enjoyment in music as being something positive to do with "spiritual apprehensions." He must mean that aesthetic emotion nurtures the spirit in some very general sense of "spirit." Again we find it on 41: "unless we can meet the new age with new methods to sustain for our populations the life of the spirit," we cannot avoid some "savage outbreak of defeated longings," making our fate like that of Russia. This is all to do with the general quality of life felt as a whole. Now I see what I want to understand. It's something like this: is there anything I feel about the importance of my music teaching that makes sense in terms of what Whitehead is discussing on page 40?

A tangent: I've just realized that I've written about a page or so without being conscious of the actual writing; it hasn't been an effort. I was just absorbed in what I wanted to get clear, and it flowed along of its own accord. Somewhere in that I sense a message for me. Perhaps at this point I should hand it over to Louise and see what she has to say about all this.

## 2. Louise Ryan's Journal

### 21 December

Jerry's difficulty about writing reminds me, by contrast, of my children, in fact, of most children I have ever known. They don't seem to have difficulty in starting and following through in practice with something which has caught their interest. The child just goes for the bricks and builds, without any paralyzing sense of someone judging whether it is going to be "right" or worthwhile. But I certainly know what Jerry means, because I am at this moment having some background anxiety about whether I will be able to say what I mean, or say anything really useful in response to Jerry.

I am thinking of the difference between the spontaneous confidence of the unharassed child and the reticence of the average adult, or adolescent, when doing what is new and challenging in more formal areas of learning, such as writing, math, science, and so on. I became curious when Jerry mentioned Whitehead's chapter on the role of classics in educating and had another look at it. And I see here that Whitehead seems to be referring to a similar issue when he says on page 70: "I often think the ruck of pupils from great English schools show a deplorable lack of intellectual zest, arising from this sense of failure." Also, looking at the pages Jerry was trying to understand, I came across this on page 38: "the schools of England have been sending up to the universities a disheartened crowd of young folk, inoculated against any outbreak of intellectual zeal." So what happens between early childhood and middle to late teenage years that changes the self-confident zest for new, difficult and challenging tasks to an attitude of fear, repulsion, and even contempt in the face of tasks of an academic or intellectual nature? Sometimes I think I can see the beginnings of this in my own children, young as they are.

I am beginning to enjoy this writing, and beginning to see why David got so obsessed with his journal, but have I ever before thought of such writing as something of importance to me? Never! I even see letters as a chore, but then I don't write my thoughts or inquire into anything in letters; I just write about what has been happening. I don't have any dialogue with friends and relatives through letters; the possibility never even occurred to me.

I've just remembered a grade two teacher of Jenny's. Jenny used to write a lot in that class, and out of it, and I was really surprised at what she could do. At a parent-teacher meeting the teacher mentioned that she followed a "whole-language" approach—I think that's what she called it. As I remember it, one key feature of this approach is that the children, no matter what is used to start them, always write something of their own, I mean, something that pops out of their own imaginations, something that comes out of an interest or experience they have had. For Jenny, it was clearly her poem or story. What struck me was not just the vitality, the special feeling in them, but the way she would just suddenly get an idea, sit down, and immediately write out the piece from start to finish. No hesitation, no fuss, no worry. Jerry seems to have kept that spirit in his music, but not in writing, as a way of expressing and expanding upon his own thoughts and feelings. But when he remembered his music, and how he proceeds with that, he suddenly saw the possibility of the same thing with writing and intellectual inquiry, and off he went! Ah! Now this is it, surely: he has confidence in his ability in music. He has done it over and over again and found that his intelligence can always come up with something worthwhile and satisfying, however many wrong turns he makes on the way. But in writing and academic subjects I gather he has been judged without being encouraged, forced rather than lured with the carrot of interest, the sense of "importance," as Whitehead would say. So he has become overly self-conscious of his capacity for error, and unaware of his capacity for successful achievement. I wonder why, in schools, making errors so easily becomes associated with failing and being a failure?

What struck me as funny was that while Jerry is writing about his mind going blank and his words drying up, he is in fact writing in quite a flowing way about this! What am I trying to get at here? It's that because he writes about what is foremost in his mind at the time, his writing starts to come easily, he gets some surprising insights, and gradually but surely finds his way to the educational issue he is looking for. Then he starts to write with equal ease about that. And he was convinced that was the very thing he could not do! What this indicates to me is that provided we start an inquiry or exploration—"learning" in that sense—written or otherwise, on a theme we have some real concern about, we can proceed with confidence and spontaneous ease. Then the real difficulties we encounter are not felt as drudgery, but more like the next hill feels to the keen hiker. In terms of our own understanding, we do then get somewhere of importance. As Jerry did. So it occurs to me that school materials, like text books, could become something other than drudgery if they were used as part of the materials for personalized learning, not as the objects of the learning. That feels good! I don't think I ever clearly realized that before.

Now I see this reference to a Dr. Green. But Jerry let his observations on his experience with her go as "a pleasant and curious oddity." He didn't really think about it; I mean, its educational implications, for example. Isn't this the very problem of being more schooled than educated? You don't have the "culture" which is "activity of thought" about what is happening to you in your everyday life. Activity of thought doesn't become a way of life, but is an occasional event. So life is divided up into the "ordinary," which you don't think about, and the "important," which you do. But the young child is not yet hampered by such arbitrary pigeon holes for putting the mind to sleep and waking it up again. He asks "Why do horses have tails?" right after asking if he can have an ice-cream, as his eyes rove from the store freezer to a picture of a horse. And when young David asked his teacher why he had to do "addings," the teacher told him just to worry about getting the answers right and not to worry his "little head" about "off-task" things. And I must admit that when I was helping in that class I accepted that comment without question. If Jerry had his natural intelligence unhindered, wouldn't he have been asking all sorts of questions about his unusual experience with Dr. Green? Why does she work differently from other professors? What is the difference between the type of learning done in her class and the kind encouraged by classes where just lectures and note-taking occur? Out of questions like these could have come some of the insights he wanted about his own teaching, if it is going to educate. I'm not being judgmental. I'm just stating the facts, or what I think they are. I remember perfectly well that in law offices I thought about where to file cases, but it never occurred to me to think about why we need lawyers, or, for that matter, why we use the same word "file" for both a folder of papers and something we shape fingernails or wood with. My schooling didn't educate me in this "activity of thought" as a way of life any more than Jerry's did.

It's just occurred to me that this could be one of the correct reasons for having a school in the first place. Parenting, peer groups, and all the other avenues of daily life don't seem to help the young person much in developing his or her "activity of thought, and receptiveness to beauty and humane feeling" as a permanent, continuous way of life. Often quite the opposite! Such activity too easily gets compartmentalized, as with Jerry and I.

I think I had better get to what would probably be considered the real "meat" of Jerry's discussion, the connection of spirit, art, vivid apprehensions of value, spiritual apprehensions, the development of the whole personality, and education. Heavens! What a mouthful! I'm all admiration for the kind of start Jerry has made with this, but where do I begin? All I can think of at the moment is an alternative to the question Jerry asked at the end of his entry. His question: "Is there anything I feel about the importance of my music teaching that makes sense in terms of what Whitehead is discussing on page 40?" I wonder if this would be better as: "Is there anything in Whitehead's discussion on page 40 that would make deeper educational sense of the importance I see in my music teaching?" I don't know, but I guess that until we have made our own sense of what Whitehead is after at the end of Chapter Three, we won't be able to tell.

For a start I firmly agree that Whitehead is not at all interested here in any religious doctrine about spirit, and is not suggesting anything which would normally be considered "religious." His interest is solidly in "educating" and the connection of that with the spirit in some broader sense. Whatever this meaning is, he seems to think the spiritual dimension of the human being is so important (to the quality of life, as Jerry puts it) that to ignore it in education is virtually to cease having education at all in any really significant sense. Now I'm stuck. I'll have to re-read those two or three pages.

It's amazing how searching with a few well aimed questions allows the text to disclose all sorts of things a mere reading keeps hidden. As I now understand it, this is how it goes. On pages 39 and 40 Whitehead is summing up what the whole chapter is about, namely, that real understanding is always reliant upon the learner's own initiative (spurred and helped by the teacher), and that initial understanding must go through cycles of the three stages if it is to emerge on higher planes. Actually, Whitehead says "higher stages of life." All right, so when we ask what kind of initiative this is, Whitehead answers that it is "the sense of value, the sense of importance." There must, then, be a feeling of enough importance in the learning if the initiative of the student is going to be able to take it onto a higher, and perhaps the highest plane, no matter how good the help given. By higher and highest planes, I am referring to higher or highest qualities of living—quality of experience is what I mean. We have to value this, or see the value it actually has, in order to have a chance, through understanding, of reaching it. But what we value here is not just something to do with our personal, or rather, egocentric interests, because, as Whitehead clearly says, the desire here is for "merging personality in something beyond itself."

Now I get my first real assurance that I know what he's getting at with "spiritual"; it has to do with becoming higher or finer by recognizing and living values which express a concern beyond preoccupation with a limited sense of self and its wants. I would call that a transcendent concern; it transcends the refusal to consider seriously only what seems to touch present self-interest. I don't know how to say that more simply. An example, perhaps, would be truth—as, say, honesty. If I am only honest when it suits what I want for myself, I do not have truth as a spiritual value. But if I feel I must be honest regardless of consequences for me, then I do have truth as a spiritual value. This sounds pompous and foreign to Whitehead's meaning, but what I mean is thoroughly down to earth. Imagine having to deal all the time with beings who could value nothing, including yourself, if it wasn't in their present self-interest! Horror stories, historical or fictional, thrive on such stuff.

The sense of "spiritual" I'm exploring here is also not moralistic, I mean, not full of disagreeable and life-denying "shoulds" and "oughts"! But it is ethical, and must be, and it also involves risk, adventure, courage. Well, take some imaginary scientists, for example. They can use their training and expertise in all sorts of ways. They can shrewdly (but I don't want to say wisely) calculate where they can work to get the most money, how to make themselves very safe in that position. And then the outcome of the work, be it medical advance or nerve gas for a mad dictator, is of little concern to them. The way they attend to truth in their work has no transcendent or spiritual quality.

But there is a completely different possibility open to them. They could find their investigations suggesting vastly different ways of regarding life, or some part of it. Such advance may be of no obvious monetary value to them or anyone else, and may invite powerful opposition from the reigning scientific establishment. If they proceed, out of the sheer transcendent passion and excitement of new frontiers in understanding, regardless of consequences for their self-interest, then truth here has this spiritual quality. I think that Einstein is generally regarded as such a person. Didn't he suffer pretty ferocious opposition when he persisted for years with his unpopular theory of relativity? Anyway, what I'm trying to counter is the idea that "spiritual" implies being a timid "yes-man," terrified of making a mistake. I sense that Whitehead has something quite different and thoroughly "beefy" in mind. In some churches I've been to I have left with the feeling that the spiritual in life is something endlessly and boringly melancholy and polite.

Is Jerry really going to plow through all this? Never mind, I have ideas coming and I must see what they are. Back to this ethical side of spiritual values and apprehensions, as I understand them. This ethical sensitivity is very demanding, but it is not moralism: the egocentric safety of following moral rules of conduct to the letter and then strutting about like a righteous, self-satisfied rooster! Be honest, don't steal, don't swear, don't live with people you aren't married to. My mother, with the best of intentions, was actually crippled by all this tame moralism.' She hardly dared to breathe! There seems no sensitivity, no intelligence in blindly following rules. Some of the groups of social, political, and ecological activists seem to me to have much more of the really spiritual or ethical values, even if they, too, can sometimes slip away into their own kinds of insensitive fanaticism. All right, what is it here that I am struggling to rescue with all these words? Let's say this: I think that when Whitehead talks the way he does of educating in relation to the spirit, he is trying to shake us awake to that side of people which is full of vitality, sensitivity, initiative, courage, and which needs to be very carefully evoked and nurtured, and is very easily killed. Now this I can get enthusiastic over.

Apologies to Jerry, but I must get down just one more idea before I lose it. When I say that this transcendent aspect of spiritual values is not a matter of a disagreeable imposition of something alien to us, I also want to say that I think it has joy and beauty in it. Today, for example, I stepped into a small gallery by mistake when I was shopping. I was just deciding to leave and get on with my list, when I became utterly lost in what struck me as a wonderful painting. I stopped thinking, forgot shopping and everything for maybe fifteen seconds, but I had no sense of how long. It could just as easily have been fifteen minutes or hours. Is that what is meant by being "transported" by beauty? Anyway, my point is that in this "getting lost," it was my normal self with all its wants and worries that I lost (for a while). So is this the transcendent, and spiritual value of beauty—or the beauty of our spiritual potential? Something like that. I have a better sense now of why Whitehead emphasizes the value of "aesthetic emotions" to the life of the spirit. What is very clear to me is the fact that I was, in those few moments, a "whole personality" in a special way. It was whole-some. All of me was caught up in the one thing and I felt so refreshed afterwards. If that is what Whitehead is making such a fuss about on page 40, then I really am listening! Over to you, Jerry, and out!

### 3. Jerry Lovett's Journal

### 23 December

I notice that we haven't been addressing each other directly in our journals, perhaps because we feel that they are journals not letters. But I realize they are also dialogue journals, so I am going to speak to you directly from now on.

About your daughter's ease of writing when it came out of her own inspiration—you said it was unmistakably hers when it was read (I think that's what you meant). I immediately thought: that's what Whitehead means by "style" in Chapter One, or at least the beginnings of it. If you do something continuously just because that's what you love to do, you develop an increasingly apparent style of your own. I don't simply mean that your signature is clearly on every aspect of the work, but that the "style" is also your special skill for effectively doing whatever it is you are trying to do. I hadn't seen this connection between personalized (non-inert) learning, its most effective expression, and the development of style. I know I'm leaping on here, but I must say I suspect that the personal identity of a style has something important to do with what Whitehead refers to as the "spirit" of a person. I can't see how to take that any further now; maybe you can.

Your assumptions about my schooling were right enough. I certainly wasn't helped to develop "activity of thought" as a way of life (as you put it). But I have trouble with the idea of activity of thought as a way of life, especially in the light of your examples. There seems to be something overdone about always questioning everything. Perhaps you don't literally mean that, but that's what it sounds like. I don't think Whitehead means constant thinking, but rather a specially honed sense of what it might be interesting and/or important to think about on any particular occasion. It's like a kind of intelligent perception that spots the interest and importance of what is normally ignored or taken for granted. And if we are educated, really, we could assume that we would be able to think effectively and fruitfully about whatever has captured our attention—you know, able to inquire into it so as to get somewhere worthwhile.

I see something else here, too, that might fit. With this mentality we would have realized that for the most part the real interest and significance of anything lies below the surface of it, and the appropriate kind of "activity of thought" is needed to dig down to find that significance. But thinking all the time? No, that sounds unbalanced and exhausting! The mind needs quiet time, or a change, like going from math to roller blades. Also it occurs to me that thinking can get in the way of feeling. I don't just mean having a feeling, but for example feeling with or for a person—empathy, compassion. Or artistic appreciation and creation—thinking about it can really interfere. Whitehead himself, on page 1, where he refers to "activity of thought," mentions "receptiveness to beauty and humane feeling." Doesn't he imply right here that thinking is to be differentiated from sensitivity to beauty and humane feeling? It also seems fairly obvious to me that if you had something like thinking separated off, without being tempered with that sensitivity, you could get conceptual monsters. Probably I could name a few! Seriously, though, just hang on to the fact that as soon as you start to think about the music you no longer hear it in a way that moves you.

You suggested that I might usefully change my basic question to: "Is there anything in Whitehead's discussion on page 40 that would make deeper educational sense of the importance I see in my music teaching?" In some ways I like the change—I mean, it avoids the danger of my simply interpreting Whitehead according to the limitations of my customary ideas of education and music teaching: But the way you have really helped me here is that now I can think of an even better question. "Is there anything in Whitehead's words which could suggest a way of teaching music that makes more educational sense than the norm?" This question demands a new way of thinking about education and about the place of music in it. So now that's what I am going to tackle.

At first I balked at your suggestion that Whitehead is implying that if the spirit is ignored we aren't going to get any education at all. However, on second thoughts, I realize I'm still reacting from a different, more obviously religious association with "spirit." There is in Whitehead's mind an important connection between his "spirit," the personality as a whole, well-being, vitality of intelligence and the wisdom of taking certain values with ultimate seriousness. By ultimate, I mean the kind of thing you were talking about in your discussion of "transcendent" values, that certain values like beauty and truth are deferred to regardless of self-interest. You got pretty sophisticated over all that, and I had to read it over several times. Although I've never really thought about anything like that before, what you said seemed to me to hold together well, for the most part. Some bits I'm doubtful about—your scientists, for example. I don't think the scientist is necessarily spiritual by loyalty to truth, even if it affects every aspect of his or her work . Ethical, yes. But wouldn't we have to know that he is loyal to truth (beauty, justice, etc.) continuously, in every area of his life, to say that he, as a person, has the spiritual as the dominant feature of himself?

Wait a minute! Are we getting confused? If we are talking about the spiritual values being dominant in every aspect of a life, aren't we talking about a saint? Whitehead is not arguing that education should be producing saints! More likely he means that enough attention to the spirit should be there if the activity is to be worthy of the name "education," in the best sense. How much is enough? That's another question altogether, and one that I don't know how to tackle. All I am sure about and want to keep clear is that although Whitehead does say in Chapter One that education should be "religious," he nowhere even nearly suggests school educators should be trying to bring about a religious transformation in young people. If he did, I could not take him seriously.

Your bit about your experience of the painting was fascinating. That really helped me with the idea of the spirit of a person, in Whitehead's sense of "a tumultuous desire for merging personality in something beyond itself" (on page 40), provided that the "something" is the right kind of thing. I mean, we all know of people merging themselves with fanatical totality in all sorts of ugly movements, inward as well as external. But with beauty, as in your example, I wouldn't (now) hesitate to say that it can readily be experienced as a spiritual value, when your whole being is taken up with it, and the sense of a separate "me" falls away. That's something to keep clear—the association of spirit and spiritual with the loss of the demands of the egocentric side of self. The transcendence of egotism, not just in the moralistic sense, but even in the sense of the delightful loss of the sense of being a lonely separate self at all! Yes, as you talk about it, I can now see why Whitehead might want to give such a high place to "aesthetic emotion" in the development of the life of the spirit. Music does it for me rather than paintings, but that's just an idiosyncratic difference.

Does Whitehead suggest that beauty has the highest spiritual value? I'm looking (on the same page) at: "The most penetrating exhibition of this force is the sense of beauty." I realize I don't even know what all the spiritual values are supposed to be. I didn't say love before, but I think that's very important, at least when it stands for compassion, affection, genuine caring. What I have no difficulty in believing is that beauty *is* a crucial spiritual value. Also, I don't like the idea of beauty excluded when there is adherence to other values. After all, can't truth be meted out in a very ugly and cruel way? Or even a very boring way? That gives me another thought: if a truth is presented in a beautiful way, it gets interesting, and then there is less likelihood of it becoming an inert idea. I like that. Is it generally recognized that the lure of beauty is a powerful motivation?

Something is clearing up for me here, around that confusion over what it takes to be a spiritual person. I haven't quite got it yet, but it involves a distinction between a spiritual person and a spiritual value (which may or may not motivate a person). My guess is that here Whitehead is interested in the effect on persons, on life, when there does happen to be a powerful response of the whole person—even for a second—to a spiritual value. There is then a potent energy, and a direction of it in a sane way beyond the limits of egocentricity. Does that sound right to you?

I wonder if the aesthetic sensitivity which can be nurtured through art, even to the point of brief transcendence, is transferable. I mean, does it flow over into a heightened appreciation of the beauty of, and thus respect for, nature, other persons, and so on? Or the beauty of a mathematical proof? Not that I can really say much on that, but I'm just wondering. My feeling is that if the sensitivity to beauty is continuously encouraged by involvement with art, it would begin to overflow into areas outside of art. Or is it that this very sensitivity would start to make life into an art? I don't mean automatically. The right kind of suggestions from the teacher would probably play an enormously important role. Anyway, I realize that Whitehead is challenging a common assumption that beauty is an ornament to life, not essential, and certainly not of great importance in teaching and learning. I have been trying to imagine life without any experience of creating and appreciating beauty. It's either horrible, unthinkable, or simply so against the way life really is that it is unimaginable. Surely educators have to think about beauty very carefully?

Now I want to tackle that question directly, because all this is giving me some ideas about it. Remember the question? Is there anything in Whitehead's words that could imply a way of teaching music which makes more educational sense than the norm? Well, I am changing my idea of teaching music to something more like educating through the teaching of music, and I challenge teachers in other curriculum areas to try something similar. It may not sound like much in words, but for me it is suggesting a fairly radical change in practice. To start with, my music teaching will be refreshment for minds that come to it tired of abstractions. So it must, whatever the approach, be enjoyable, not necessarily "fun," but interesting, moving, engaging. I have thought of myself as reasonably good on this score, but I am now getting a sense of an art of teaching here that I have barely begun to explore. It has to be educational though; not just a good time. From the discussions and my exchange with you, I would say that implies "keeping knowledge alive" (as opposed to inert ideas), and that means there have to be explorations, inquiries, which are somewhat personally shaped. So instead of giving students all the information about music theory, history, performance, etc., I shall try finding ways to help them discover these things for themselves. As I understand Chapter Five, a guiding principle that I shall now have very consciously before me is "learning by contact," involving individual contact with instruments, tapes, records, disks, books, scores, and devising joint productions to perform for each other in addition to the occasional public performances. I am asking myself questions like: why shouldn't those who enjoy drama explore and dramatically depict the life of a musician? Why shouldn't those with a flare for creative writing produce their own poems and stories to be read with the heightened effect of self-created or carefully selected music? Why shouldn't mathematically-inclined students explore the structure of Bach's compositional style? All this is really just applying to music teaching Whitehead's example in Chapter One of the combination of geography, history and mathematics in practical projects.

I also have to rethink the music curriculum itself. On page 36, I see that Whitehead is emphatic that time and energy for the unpredictable wanderings of "romantic interest" will not be there if the predictable parts—"what the pupil has got to know in precise fashion"—are not clearly worked out in the teacher's mind. In other words, I can't waste our time on inessentials. That would be the mistake of "reconditeness" he discusses in Chapter Six. What Whitehead doesn't say here, though the whole book is about it, is that part of what teachers must get clear about "essentials only" is their own ideas of what is essential for educating as such, whatever the age, subject, and so on. And they must be clear about what really doesn't help, what positively hinders. That's basically what we have been doing together with Whitehead as catalyst, isn't it, Louise?

Here I must stop. There are still Christmas gifts to be bought and wrapped, and a dozen other things clamoring for my attention. Happy Christmas to you and your family. Buy David a beautiful journal and an italic pen!

# Ten

# THIRD EXCHANGE OF JOURNALS: DAVID
# AND CRAIG

## 1. David Ryan's Journal

### 14 December

The more I reflect on everything we've talked over as a group, the more I think Whitehead is proposing things far more radical than we realized. He is proposing changes which are not mere alterations in the details of school procedures, but changes in the basic structure of schooling as we know it. There would be enormous resistance to that, since there are too many vested interests and immovable habits of thought which don't like big changes. I don't want to go into that now. I had better just see whether my intuition stands up or not.

On page 29, Whitehead says, "so long as we conceive intellectual education as merely consisting in the acquirement of mechanical mental aptitudes, and of formulated statements of useful truths, there can be no progress." So far as I can see, with a few exceptions here and there, that's more or less how schools and universities still regard their task. Then Whitehead goes on to say, "there will be much activity, amid aimless re-arrangement of syllabuses, in the fruitless endeavor to dodge the inevitable lack of time." Leaving the issue of time aside, he seems to be suggesting that only radically reconceiving schooling, or any institutionalized education, will really allow for the kind of teaching and learning he is advocating.

I was struck by the truth of what he says about examinations, how education is ruined when the teaching comes to be governed by what will be on the exams. What would genuinely educational teaching be aiming at? He states it succinctly on page 5: "The evocation of curiosity, of judgment, of the power of mastering a complicated tangle of circumstances, the use of theory in giving foresight in special cases. . . ." Then he states an obvious truth that nonetheless doesn't seem to be so obvious since we still act as if it weren't true: "all these powers are not to be imparted by a set rule embodied in one schedule of examination subjects."

Again, if we take seriously the encouragement of creative initiative, there must be adequate regard for the individuality of the person and the context of learning. Creative intelligence is intensely individual. When I have that in mind, I understand immediately Whitehead's point about external examinations: "no educational system is possible unless every question asked of a pupil at any examination is either framed or modified by the actual teacher of that pupil in that subject." The curriculum subject is so differently dealt with by each teacher, and so differently engaged in by each different class and student. And so it should be, since they are all different. But if you teach to an external exam written entirely by some outside person or committee, you have to try and teach everyone in the same way, which is impossible, and so the very attempt distorts the whole process.

I also see why Whitehead says "no educational system is possible." I think it implies that we can have a system with the examinations he criticizes (and we do have it!), but it won't truly be educational. This is radical talk! And he leaves me in no doubt whatsoever now about this when I read on page 13:

> Each school should grant its own leaving certificates, based on its own curriculum. The standards of these schools should be sampled and corrected. But the first requisite for educational reform is the school as a unit, with its approved curriculum based on its own needs, and evolved by its own staff.

What if we don't? He tells us a few lines on. "If we fail to secure that, we simply fall from one formalism into another, from one dung-hill of inert ideas into another." So he is arguing that if we are to secure what educating is primarily about—alive, not inert, minds and ideas—changes in the system as a whole must be made.

So what do I get from this? It's not enough to clarify and modify our ideas about the details of day-to-day teaching and learning. That's crucial, and that's what we began in our group dialogues. But the added point now pushing in on me—one I don't know how to deal with—is that all the changes we talked over will be continually thwarted in action if there aren't some overall system changes towards a fundamentally different schooling and university. This boggles my mind—that we have spent more than a century in public schooling building up the kind of system that actually makes real educating almost impossible! Over to you, Craig. I don't know how to go on from here.

## 2. Craig Stonehouse's Journal

### 13 December

Knowing my interest in science I suppose, Henry dropped a nice little bombshell into my hands as we were leaving the other night—a book by Whitehead called *Science and the Modern World*. I haven't been able to put it down. I've never read a critical exploration of the development of scientific ideas like this before. Why this was never studied in any of my years of science courses I can't imagine! My science education almost entirely missed out this intriguing history and philosophy of science—the story of the whole enterprise.

Whitehead is always thinking about things differently from the mainstream, and ending a book on science with an essay on "Requisites for Social Progress" is no exception. What has my attention right now is all the educational stuff in this essay. If you have the Free Press edition, look at page 198. For me it was just as he says here:

My own criticism of our traditional educational methods is that they are far too much occupied with intellectual analysis, and with the acquirement of formularized information . . . we neglect to strengthen habits of concrete appreciation of the individual facts in their full interplay of emergent values, and . . . merely emphasize abstract formulations which ignore this aspect of the interplay of diverse values.

If I understand Whitehead, a couple of things come strongly to mind here. In the way I was taught, we were rarely encouraged to look at things ourselves so as to make our own scientific sense of them. We had to focus immediately on what some expert had interpreted and theorized, and then our experimentation was mainly to get results which have already been determined. And we never looked at the experts themselves—their lives, their social context, everything which led them to discover what all the others hadn't even thought to examine. Is this what Whitehead means by "concrete appreciation"? Mostly, what we get is a lot of abstractions floating around in abstract space.

And look further down the page. I really like this: "In the Garden of Eden Adam saw the animals before he named them: in the traditional system, children named the animals before they saw them." That's it, in a nutshell! So one of his main points is, I think, that all this ungrounded abstraction (which makes for a lot of inert ideas) leads to a very one-sided development. At the top of the page Whitehead adds something to his talk of wisdom in *The Aims* (and seems to suggest it's the central or definitive aim of educating). He says: "Wisdom is the fruit of balanced development. It is this balanced growth of individuality which it should be the aim of education to secure."

Somewhere in here fits the issue of values—in fact I see I've quoted Whitehead on the "interplay of diverse values." I had to learn whatever I have learned about the social and political values influencing science on my own, and Whitehead's exploration of this shows how little I've learned. Why shouldn't it be considered crucial, and fascinating, to see how science has been affected by what he calls "the watchwords of the nineteenth century"? What are they? Whitehead lays them out on page 205. The "struggle for existence, competition, class warfare, commercial antagonism between nations, military warfare." He associates all this with what he calls a "gospel of hate." The Darwinian notion of the struggle for existence—the survival of the fittest— has, it seems from this discussion, filtered over into political and commercial life so that savage competition is the dominant value. Whoever perishes in the struggle, well, too bad, they weren't fit enough! But isn't this also the way institutional education functions? My schooling was competitive through and through, and university still is. And literally, if you can't make the grade, you have to fall by the wayside regardless of your desire to carry on your education. Even if you do carry on, is this atmosphere of competition a good thing for educating? Mostly it seems to me that it creates fear, anxiety, resentment, and cruel ambition.

Something else in this essay reminds me of Whitehead's emphasis on respecting the natural way that understanding comes about. Here, talking of Social Darwinism, he argues that it is based on an unbalanced view of nature, where competition is seen as dominant. In fact, he argues at length, in an examination of forests, that sustained life requires the dominant law to be that of "association," "cooperation." Now, a lovely quote from page 206. "Every organism acquires an environment of friends. . . . The Gospel of Force [antagonism] is incompatible with a social life." An environment of friends! I like that. And it's true. We are all interdependent beings, and our survival, health, and sanity depend on collaboration. That is the natural law. And that is what the schools go against. Why aren't we encouraged to learn in a collaborative way, all helping each other, working together? Take our recent discussions as an example, where we were working together in dialogue to understand Whitehead and what we are doing in education. It was enjoyable, alive, fruitful. Isn't that the way learning ought to be for human beings? We were "an environment of friends!" What all this seems to amount to, in my mind at least, is that school and university have wrong and dangerous values in their very foundation. The whole foundation needs changing. No wonder Whitehead has not been followed. He's a revolutionary, and they aren't liked in a firmly established society.

### 3. Craig Stonehouse's Journal

#### 16 December

Good heavens, David! I've just got your journal entry of 14 December, and find that you have arrived at the same conclusion as I have. We were both pursuing an essentially similar line of thought at the same time. But now I've seen the material you use, it adds to mine, and I feel even more strongly that to subscribe to a Whiteheadian kind of outlook in education implies a call for radical, systemic changes—and not just in practical organization, but in our basic understanding of what "educating" should mean.

What I want to add now is some of my thoughts about university education. After my last journal entry I started thinking about my own university experience, and that drew me back to reread Whitehead's chapter on universities in *The Aims*. Just a few things that stand out for me. Listen to this (page 93): "So far as the mere imparting of information is concerned, no university has had any justification for existence since the popularization of printing in the fifteenth century." That's so obvious for students who have books and can read, and yet we've missed it. Think of the interminable lectures which are little more than an imparting of information that's already in the books! Then on the same page he goes on to say what he thinks the purpose of a university is: "The justification for a university is that it preserves the connection between knowledge and the zest of life, by uniting the young and the old in the imaginative consideration of learning." Now is that an environment of friends in learning or isn't it? And I can see that this is his way of elaborating what he said in earlier chapters about universities being predominantly a big "generalization" stage of learning—ideally. In their research, they are at this stage, but not in their teaching. So his view is that the real educational purpose of university teaching is not just to impart yet more information, but to teach the students to generalize the information imaginatively so as to see life in a new, and truer light. In my experience a few professors do this, but most do not do it at all. Overall, the university isn't regarded this way. It's more just an extension of school, and the wrong sort of schooling at that! Why, we students even refer to university as "school."

In this chapter, Whitehead seems to be arguing that the universities are "homes of adventure shared in common by young and old" (page 98), where the adventure is, amongst other things, about values. He thinks it is here that the true values of being a "civilized" culture should be clarified, and brought to life all over again by being applied to every area of life as it is now. I can see how necessary this is, since the results of the barbaric Social Darwinism are everywhere to see. And as I think about this, if the universities, which are best equipped to do this, don't do it, who will? And if no one does it, what kind of life, globally, can we expect in the future?

I phoned up Henry and discussed some of these ideas with him. He said that he largely agreed with me, and that Whitehead was deeply concerned about "civilized values" and had written a whole section on them in his *Adventures of Ideas*. Henry said that there Whitehead lists the civilized values as truth, beauty, art, peace, and adventure, and that once you know this you can see that ultimately the working out of them in daily life is his main concern in everything he says about education. This makes a lot of sense to me. After all, if, as an educator, you couldn't justify your practice as contributing to the realization of these values, how could you justify it at all? What values, what quality of life, would you be contributing to? What do you think?

# Eleven

# FOURTH EXCHANGE OF JOURNALS: ANNE AND MARIA

### 1. Anne MacLean's Journal

### 14 December

One thing burning a hole in my notes is a connection I want to work out be-tween "soul murder" (page 57) and the essence of education as "religious" (page 14). Both of these are scandalous passages (to an agnostic like me) and, I suspect, more far-reaching than anything I have ever thought about regarding education. And that's a combination I simply can't resist. I hope you can get interested in this, Maria, because I cannot start with anything more "normal" than this. So, good-bye to my thesis for an hour or so! Please, Maria, reply to my ideas plainly, frankly, and don't bother to be polite; you know I can't stand withholding, pretending, and generally beating around the bush.

My idea is this: when Whitehead refers to soul murder, he is in the mid-dle of a discussion of the teaching of literature. He says (on page 57): "Literature only exists to express and develop the imaginative world which is our life, the kingdom which is within us," and then goes on to point out that if you destroy the enjoyment of it, literature can't fulfill this purpose. So "our life," "the kingdom which is within us," is being harmed by teaching without this enjoyment. Murdered? Is that too strong? I'm not sure, but it does follow that if life is being harmed it is on the way to being threatened with extinc-tion. Harm is a stage on the way towards death. Reduce my oxygen enough and you harm me. Keep reducing it and you kill me. Though this is the life "within," right? Anyway, if not soul murder, soul death at least seems to be a logical conclusion if the teaching is continuously wrong.

As I understand his language, the "soul" is a source of special energy at the center of the person, like the spring which gives birth to the river and the whole landscape it sustains. Or, drying up, leaves a stagnant swamp, and fi-nally, a desert. "Imaginative" in the quote seems to mean the energy or passion of initiative, creativity, discovery, intrinsic to "soul"—the riches of this "kingdom."

Why does Whitehead say "our life" is the kingdom within? What about everything without, outside, which is part of our lives? I make sense of this when I ask where the quality of life as we feel it (joyful, painful, monotonous, and so on) is. We aren't surrounded by qualities of life as we are surrounded by trees, walls, and so on. Quality of this sort is only felt by a someone. It is always the quality of some being's "within." I may say to you that you have a substantial income and a lovely house and family, implying that you have a good quality of life. But if for whatever reasons you feel awful in the midst of all this, in fact you do not have a good quality of life. Your kingdom is within and the treasury may be locked up, burgled, dwindled away frivolously to nothing, or even lost!

That was a mouthful, I know, Maria, but without explaining that I can't go on. You'll see. Stay with me! Right. Onward! The state of the "kingdom within" is Whitehead's concern, especially in so far as "educating" implies the freeing and strengthening of this kingdom by adventure into and with the world of ideas. But the state of this kingdom within is most definitely the concern, par excellence, of any religion worth the name. So, without going overboard, and saying something as silly as education is religion, one can say without absurdity that the essence of education is that it be religious, as Whitehead does on page 14. At the moment I'm not agreeing or disagreeing; I'm just trying to understand what Whitehead is after in all this. Then I can see what I want to use of it.

What is the overlap, then, between religious development and the kind of personal development education should assist? And if there isn't this particular overlap, why will all attempts to educate—in the wisest sense—be but poor copies of the real thing? Whitehead's answer? Something to do with duty and reverence (same page). "A religious education inculcates duty and reverence." Note that he doesn't say "being taught religion" or "being taught to be religious." He says, "a religious education." Big difference.

Let's start with "duty," as arising "from our potential control over the course of events," such that "where attainable knowledge could have changed the course of events, ignorance has the guilt of vice." I think Whitehead is taking the cause and effect basis of life very seriously, and pointing out that our degree of understanding has quite definite consequences—for ourselves and for those with whom we have contact. To ignore that is to pretend we are not responsible where in fact we are. If we take responsibility, we make sure we attempt to know everything we can to help bring about what is best in any situation. So what is at issue here, in education or any other walk of life, is the necessity for informed and intelligent foresight. In religion, to ignore or reject this responsibility is, I suppose, "sin." In education, it is a "vice." Both imply unnecessarily bringing about bad consequences. Let others haggle over the differences and similarities of sin and vice. Both involve a lack of a special type of caring which is essential to the health of the "soul," the "kingdom within"—of oneself and of others. So this is one overlap between religious concern and educational concern.

Now let's look at "reverence" on page 14. This is a tough one! "The foundation of reverence is this perception, that the present holds within itself the complete sum of existence, backwards and forwards, that whole amplitude of time, which is eternity." I hesitate here because I know Whitehead is expressing something he has gone into very deeply, and which I have barely begun to think about. But this is part of his talk to educators, so I think I ought to be able to get something useful out of it. At any rate, I am going to have a crack at it! All right, he is suggesting we have this special attitude of reverence in what we are doing if we understand the peculiar fact of the present holding all of existence, past and future, within itself. If it is true, it is already rather an awesome fact to contemplate, and awe is, I would think, a kind of reverence—a standing back in wonder at something.

That discussion we had, about ways in which the future and past exist in the present, helps somewhat here, so my mind is not completely blank in front of a statement which flies right in the face of what we normally assume—that past, present, and future are quite separate. I mean, I can see that the very idea of foresight implies that we can already have in our minds something of the shape of the future. Just using a bus timetable and then going and catching the bus is an example of that. But that seems rather trivial. Or is that the point—that in the present one can imagine both trivial and profound things to shape the future? So then we would revere the present as being a place where all sorts of marvelous or terrible possibilities exist, and we can pass right through it without a thought for all this! Is this why, on page 3, Whitehead says the present is holy ground? I see he is pointing out here that "The only use of a knowledge of the past is to equip us for the present," and presumably also then the future. I don't recall history being presented to me as having any message for me in the present—so it wasn't really present-ed, was it, Maria? Have you ever really thought about the meaning of that verb "to present?" I hadn't, until a moment ago. I mean, in the sense of "to make present," that is, "to make important in and to the present." We keep talking about "presenting" things in our teaching, but the important meaning of this is ignored.

If I revere something, I regard it as in some way sacred. What would change if I regarded the present as sacred? I'm sure I can only scratch the surface here, but at least that is a start. I think I would begin asking questions like: what is the quality of my present—and of those I am influencing? What is the quality of the present of my students? How has my past and the past in general affected this quality of my present, and so my future and that of others? Am I learning anything important about that past so as to be able to overcome some of its limitations on my present? (I won't say "and the future" again, because when future events exist, they will be the new present!) Are my students presently experiencing anything really worthwhile? Because if they aren't, the poverty of this present of theirs will seriously limit what they can realize in present moments to come. A dead present puts a dead hand on the future. So if, as an educator, I inculcate reverence in Whitehead's sense, I am attempting to help them to take the present seriously, through everything I do with them. No, more than that. Through what I am with them. I am attempting to help them to have each present as a rich experience. I can see why Whitehead puts duty and reverence together. Reverence is the attitude where something of great value is recognized, and duty is the action which honors that value.

## 2. Maria Vanzelli's Journal

### 17 December

I had no idea how to start until I got your journal, Anne, and I'm a bit awed by the way you think. It looks so much more impressive than anything I know how to write. Quite a lot of it I had to read several times to get your meaning, but in some places it sounded like poetry, and I understood immediately. When you talked of soul as an inner spring which gives birth to a river, or dries up into a swamp or a desert, it made sense right away to me. I thought of times when I have been utterly exhausted at the end of a kindergarten day, and feel as if I shall never find any energy or inspiration again. And yet the children are still full of energy. I look at the faces of the parents when they come to get their children, and some are always bright and cheerful, but some are always withdrawn and depressed, as if their spring has almost dried up. That worries me, though not half as much as when I occasionally have children like that, so full of anxiety, or gone off inside themselves somewhere to escape. If these are what Whitehead refers to as alive or dying souls, I have to agree that it's terribly serious to understand how to encourage aliveness to stay, or to come back, through fun or, better still, through the kind of enjoyment where people can forget everything in the intense interest of what they are doing.

What you said about the meaning of "presenting" something, stressing that the word implies making something present, was clever. When the children are bored or too anxious to get involved, the present for them is a desert, or a dangerous jungle! I can see why they act up when they are bored. They have to get some life into their present, don't they? When I present an idea or project to them, am I really making it present for them? That's a way of putting the challenge I had never thought of before, and yet with the question put like that I can see right away what the heart of it all is. I mean, I don't think anything useful happens for them if the present doesn't interest them. And I can see that if this happens over and over, eventually they will be like the adolescents I see who can't find anything of interest in school at all. In fact, eventually, they will be like those parents who look so constantly depressed or troubled.

That thought made me wonder about the tendency of a lot of people to see kindergarten mainly as a preparation for grade one. You know, then the important thing is for them to be obedient, be able to sit still at a task, know their letters and numbers, and so on. Actually, it made me think of how I have so often fallen into that. Then I try to make them learn letters and numbers even if they hate it, or I cunningly slip number ideas into every conversation or activity even when I can see that they find it irrelevant. I don't like that, because I'm deceiving them, pretending I'm just playing with them, but really trying to push their play towards what I think they ought to be learning. Thinking about Whitehead's inert ideas as harmful, and what he calls "soul murder," makes me realize that I'm not going to do that any more. After all, what does it mean to be prepared for grade one if the child can add numbers but hates learning, is mostly unhappy, and is getting afraid to try anything in case of making a mistake?

I just thought that maybe this is what you are getting at with "reverence." I have decided I must have more reverence for the child's feelings. Well, no, it's more than that. I realize I do have that kind of respect and love for the children, and that from now on I am not going to be argued out of it, and persuaded to go against it. I see that when I do, I become unhappy too, and Henry had a good point when he said that teachers should respect themselves and be sure that their teaching is good for themselves. The tiredness at the end of a busy day I get over with a good night's sleep, but not that peculiar anxiety I have when I let myself be persuaded to teach in ways that I can see are not good for the children. What you say about the past, present and future—and what Whitehead says—makes some sense to me now. Whatever is supposed to be good for the children has got to be good for them right now. Not just that we say that it is good, but it has to feel good to the children themselves. It has to make sense to them now. It has to feel interesting to them now. Imagine a five- or six-year-old being motivated by being told that this or that will be good for them in grade one next year! Well, I don't want to go overboard. Not everything they have to do can feel good to them, but we have to aim to let everything that can be experienced as enjoyable. I guess you would say that we have a duty to do that, and to find out how to do that more. What I'm realizing is that I have taken enjoyment too much for granted. Would you say that enjoyment to the soul or spirit is like oxygen to the body? I wouldn't have spoken like this three months ago, but right now that seems to make perfect sense to me.

So enjoyment is a precious thing, to be nurtured, protected, encouraged. Never to be taken for granted, and its absence never to be ignored. It certainly must not be obscured by silly talk of everything needing to be "fun" for children. That's the main idea for me right now, and I think I shall just stop there. One question, though, before I stop. Do you enjoy writing your thesis, Anne? I never thought to ask you before.

Wait, I forgot to tell you one more thing. Do you remember I told you after some of our group discussions that my dissatisfaction with myself as a teacher seemed to come from realizing that I started (but couldn't carry through) teaching with a few good methods and a few half-understood early childhood education ideas? Well, somewhere in my mind I have been looking for some words that would really capture a vision of everything I would deeply love to be as a teacher. Now I have found them, and every time I read them, I have such a strong feeling of my own vision, and all it implies for what I think is the profound meaning of "enjoyment" for my practice and for the children's whole experience of school. In light of all the group has explored together this saying gives me more of a feeling of being on utterly solid ground educationally than I have ever felt. The words are Whitehead's, on pages 39 and 40 of *The Aims*. It now sounds as if I said the words myself. (I forgive the "him" since I know he was writing in a time when this form was accepted as gender neutral.)

> The teacher has a double function. It is for him to elicit the enthusiasm by resonance from his own personality, and to create the environment of a larger knowledge and a firmer purpose. He is there to avoid the waste, which in the lower stages of existence is nature's way of evolution. The ultimate motive power, alike in science, in morality, and in religion, is the sense of value, the sense of importance. It takes the various forms of wonder, of curiosity, of reverence, or worship, of tumultuous desire for merging personality in something beyond itself. This sense of value imposes on life incredible labours, and apart from it life sinks back into its lower types. The most penetrating exhibition of this force is the sense of beauty, the aesthetic sense of realized perfection.

I keep thinking I've finished, and then what I've written leads to something else. Is that the growing breadth of knowledge or understanding we talked about in the discussions? Understanding spreading out, one thing leading to another? Anyway, my idea now is this: just as I was thinking Whitehead's main idea is enjoyment, it occurred to me that it might be the sense of beauty. But it doesn't have to be one or the other, does it? Isn't enjoyment, if it is present, the beauty in being alive? I think it is, and then I think that hindering enjoyment is unnecessarily making life ugly.

That leads me to another idea (my last, I promise). I hardly know how to say it, but here goes. I think Whitehead was suggesting, to all of us involved with educating, that we have a responsibility that is different, and much, much bigger, than we usually suppose. It's not just a horrible burden of a responsibility, because it is also an opportunity, and a marvelous one. It is an opportunity much, much more exciting than the best satisfaction of teaching as we normally think of it. You see, the school years come in the most impressionable period of people's lives, when they are developing themselves in ways that will be with them for a lifetime. Imagine, then, that we have the opportunity in those years to help establish, for someone's whole life, the feeling of the beauty in being alive simply as what we basically are—human. How? By making it the foremost purpose of all school life to evoke the enjoyment that is present only when the mind is alive with the activity most true to its nature.

# WORKS CITED

Abbott, Edwin A. (1986) *Flatland*. Harmondsworth, England: Penguin Books.

Dearden, R.F., P.H. Hirst, R.S. Peters (eds.). (1972) *Education and the Development of Reason*. London and Boston: Routledge and Kegan Paul.

Dewey, John. (1916) *Democracy and Education*. New York: Macmillan Publishing Co. Inc.

Hamilton, Edith and Huntington Cairns (eds.). (1961) *The Collected Dialogues of Plato including the Letters*. Princeton, N. J.: Princeton University Press.

Hawkins, David. (1965) "Messing around in Science," *Science and Children* (February).

Hinton, E. (1904) *The Fourth Dimension*. London, George Allen.

Illich, Ivan. (1971) *Deschooling Society*. New York: Harper and Row.

Johnson, A.H. (ed.). (1959) *Whitehead's American Essays in Social Philosophy*. New York: Harper and Brothers.

_____. (ed.). (1961) *Alfred North Whitehead: The Interpretation of Science; Selected Essays*. Indianapolis, New York: Liberal Arts Press, The Bobbs-Merrill Company.

Matthews, Gareth B. (1984) *Dialogues with Children*. Cambridge, Mass. and London: Harvard University Press.

O'Hear, Anthony. (1981) *Education, Society, and Human Nature: An Introduction to the Philosophy of Education*. London, Boston, and Henley: Routledge and Kegan Paul.

Price, Lucien. (ed.). (1956) *Dialogues of Alfred North Whitehead*. New York: Mentor Books.

Roszak, Theodore. (1986) *The Cult of Information: The Folklore of Computers and the True Art of Thinking*. New York: Pantheon Books, Random House, Inc.

Schilpp, Paul Arthur. (ed.). (1951) *The Philosophy of Alfred North Whitehead*. LaSalle, Ill.: Open Court.

Whitehead, Alfred North. (1958) *An Introduction to Mathematics*. London, Oxford, New York: Oxford University Press.

_____. (1960) *Religion in the Making*. New York and Cleveland: Meridian Books, The World Publishing Company.

146                *Works Cited*

_____. (1967) *Adventures of Ideas*. New York: Free Press.

_____. (1967) *The Aims of Education and other Essays*. New York: The Free Press.

_____. (1967) *Science and the Modern World*. New York: The Free Press.

_____. (1968) *Modes of Thought*. New York: The Free Press.

_____. (1978) *Process and Reality: An Essay in Cosmology*, Corrected Edition, ed. David Ray Griffin and Donald W. Sherburne. New York: The Free Press.

# ABOUT THE AUTHOR

Foster N. Walker was born in England in 1941. In 1963 he left industrial chemical research to train as an elementary school teacher, and from 1966 to 1971 he taught in British and Canadian elementary schools. After obtaining his B.A. in English Literature and B.A.Hons. in Philosophy at the University of Winnipeg, Manitoba, he completed doctoral studies in philosophy at The University of Western Ontario. In 1976 he taught in the philosophy department of The University of Winnipeg and in the same year moved to a permanent position teaching philosophy of education in The Department of Educational Foundations of The University of Alberta. In 1979 he was awarded a doctorate in philosophy for his thesis, *Knowing and Education: An Epistemological Perspective on Whitehead's Educational Theory*. He formed and co-facilitated the Edmonton Large Dialogue Group in 1991 and the Calgary Large Dialogue Group in 1994, continuing the experimentation with dialogue in the large group begun by Patrick deMaré and by David Bohm. In 1996 he left university work as Professor Emeritus to focus on writing and on researching dialogue as the unique and most unfamiliar potential of human speech and relationship.

Foster N. Walker has given numerous lectures and workshops for school and university teachers. He has made experimental teaching in the university a continuing area of practical research and the basis of articles and conference papers on school and university pedagogy. His unpublished book manuscript on philosophy of education, *Education with a Human Face*, was for many years used with students of education at the University of Alberta. He has published articles in philosophy of education and delivered papers at conferences on philosophy and the philosophy of education in Canada, England, and the United States. Many of these have involved the educational implications of the philosophies of Alfred North Whitehead and Jiddu Krishnamurti, and the significance of dialogue for education. He is a past president of The Northwest Philosophy of Education Society. He is presently facilitating a philosophy dialogue group in Calgary, Alberta, and writing a novel that explores the process of large dialogue groups and the effect of dialogue in everyday life.

# INDEX

**VIBS**

The **Value Inquiry Book Series** is co-sponsored by:

American Maritain Association
American Society for Value Inquiry
Association for Process Philosophy of Education
Center for Bioethics, University of Turku
Center for International Partnerships, Rochester Institute of Technology
Center for Professional and Applied Ethics, University of North Carolina at
Charlotte
Centre for Applied Ethics, Hong Kong Baptist University
Centre for Cultural Research, Aarhus University
College of Education and Allied Professions, Bowling Green State University
Concerned Philosophers for Peace
Conference of Philosophical Societies
Global Association for the Study of Persons
Institute of Philosophy of the High Council of Scientific Research, Spain
International Academy of Philosophy of the Principality of Liechtenstein
International Society for Universal Dialogue
Natural Law Society
Philosophical Society of Finland
Philosophy Born of Struggle Association
Philosophy Seminar, University of Mainz
R.S. Hartman Institute for Formal and Applied Axiology
Russian Philosophical Society
Society for Iberian and Latin-American Thought
Society for the Philosophic Study of Genocide and the Holocaust
Society for the Philosophy of Sex and Love
Yves R. Simon Institute.

## Titles Published

1. Noel Balzer, *The Human Being as a Logical Thinker.*

2. Archie J. Bahm, *Axiology: The Science of Values.*

3. H. P. P. (Hennie) Lötter, *Justice for an Unjust Society.*

4. H. G. Callaway, *Context for Meaning and Analysis: A Critical Study in the Philosophy of Language.*

5. Benjamin S. Llamzon, *A Humane Case for Moral Intuition.*

6. James R. Watson, *Between Auschwitz and Tradition: Postmodern Reflections on the Task of Thinking.* A volume in **Holocaust and Genocide Studies.**

7. Robert S. Hartman, *Freedom to Live: The Robert Hartman Story, edited by Arthur R. Ellis.* A volume in **Hartman Institute Axiology Studies.**

8. Archie J. Bahm, *Ethics: The Science of Oughtness.*

9. George David Miller, *An Idiosyncratic Ethics; Or, the Lauramachean Ethics.*

10. Joseph P. DeMarco, *A Coherence Theory in Ethics.*

11. Frank G. Forrest, *Valuemetrics^N: The Science of Personal and Professional Ethics.* A volume in **Hartman Institute Axiology Studies.**

12. William Gerber, *The Meaning of Life: Insights of the World's Great Thinkers.*

13. Richard T. Hull, Editor, *A Quarter Century of Value Inquiry: Presidential Addresses of the American Society for Value Inquiry.* A volume in **Histories and Addresses of Philosophical Societies.**

14. William Gerber, *Nuggets of Wisdom from Great Jewish Thinkers: From Biblical Times to the Present.*

15. Sidney Axinn, *The Logic of Hope: Extensions of Kant's View of Religion.*

16. Messay Kebede, *Meaning and Development.*

17. Amihud Gilead, *The Platonic Odyssey: A Philosophical-Literary Inquiry into the Phaedo.*

18. Necip Fikri Alican, *Mill's Principle of Utility: A Defense of John Stuart Mill's Notorious Proof.* A volume in **Universal Justice**.

19. Michael H. Mitias, Editor, *Philosophy and Architecture.*

20. Roger T. Simonds, *Rational Individualism: The Perennial Philosophy of Legal Interpretation.* A volume in **Natural Law Studies**.

21. William Pencak, *The Conflict of Law and Justice in the Icelandic Sagas.*

22. Samuel M. Natale and Brian M. Rothschild, Editors, *Values, Work, Education: The Meanings of Work.*

23. N. Georgopoulos and Michael Heim, Editors, *Being Human in the Ultimate: Studies in the Thought of John M. Anderson.*

24. Robert Wesson and Patricia A. Williams, Editors, *Evolution and Human Values.*

25. Wim J. van der Steen, *Facts, Values, and Methodology: A New Approach to Ethics.*

26. Avi Sagi and Daniel Statman, *Religion and Morality.*

27. Albert William Levi, *The High Road of Humanity: The Seven Ethical Ages of Western Man*, edited by Donald Phillip Verene and Molly Black Verene.

28. Samuel M. Natale and Brian M. Rothschild, Editors, *Work Values: Education, Organization, and Religious Concerns.*

29. Laurence F. Bove and Laura Duhan Kaplan, Editors, *From the Eye of the Storm: Regional Conflicts and the Philosophy of Peace.* A volume in **Philosophy of Peace.**

30. Robin Attfield, *Value, Obligation, and Meta-Ethics.*

31. William Gerber, *The Deepest Questions You Can Ask About God: As Answered by the World's Great Thinkers.*

32. Daniel Statman, *Moral Dilemmas.*

33. Rem B. Edwards, Editor, *Formal Axiology and Its Critics.* A volume in **Hartman Institute Axiology Studies.**

34. George David Miller and Conrad P. Pritscher, *On Education and Values: In Praise of Pariahs and Nomads.* A volume in **Philosophy of Education.**

35. Paul S. Penner, *Altruistic Behavior: An Inquiry into Motivation.*

36. Corbin Fowler, *Morality for Moderns.*

37. Giambattista Vico, *The Art of Rhetoric (Institutiones Oratoriae,* 1711-1741), from the definitive Latin text and notes, Italian commentary and introduction by Giuliano Crifo, translated and edited by Giorgio A. Pinton and Arthur W. Shippee. A volume in **Values in Italian Philosophy.**

38. W. H. Werkmeister, *Martin Heidegger on the Way,* edited by Richard T. Hull. A volume in **Werkmeister Studies.**

39. Phillip Stambovsky, *Myth and the Limits of Reason.*

40. Samantha Brennan, Tracy Isaacs, and Michael Milde, Editors, *A Question of Values: New Canadian Perspectives in Ethics and Political Philosophy.*

41. Peter A. Redpath, *Cartesian Nightmare: An Introduction to Transcendental Sophistry.* A volume in **Studies in the History of Western Philosophy.**

42. Clark Butler, *History as the Story of Freedom: Philosophy in Intercultural Context,* with Responses by sixteen scholars.

43. Dennis Rohatyn, *Philosophy History Sophistry.*

44. Leon Shaskolsky Sheleff, *Social Cohesion and Legal Coercion: A Critique of Weber, Durkheim, and Marx.* Afterword by Virginia Black.

45. Alan Soble, Editor, *Sex, Love, and Friendship: Studies of the Society for the Philosophy of Sex and Love, 1977-1992.* A volume in **Histories and Addresses of Philosophical Societies.**

46. Peter A. Redpath, *Wisdom's Odyssey: From Philosophy to Transcendental Sophistry.* A volume in **Studies in the History of Western Philosophy.**

47. Albert A. Anderson, *Universal Justice: A Dialectical Approach.* A volume in **Universal Justice.**

48. Pio Colonnello, *The Philosophy of Jose Gaos.* Translated from Italian by Peter Cocozzella. Edited by Myra Moss. Introduction by Giovanni Gullace. A volume in **Values in Italian Philosophy.**

49. Laura Duhan Kaplan and Laurence F. Bove, Editors, Philosophical Perspectives on Power and Domination: Theories and Practices. A volume in **Philosophy of Peace.**

50. Gregory F. Mellema, *Collective Responsibility.*

51. Josef Seifert, *What Is Life? The Originality, Irreducibility, and Value of Life.* A volume in **Central-European Value Studies.**

52. William Gerber, *Anatomy of What We Value Most.*

53. Armando Molina, *Our Ways: Values and Character*, edited by Rem B. Edwards. A volume in **Hartman Institute Axiology Studies.**

54. Kathleen J. Wininger, *Nietzsche's Reclamation of Philosophy.* A volume in **Central-European Value Studies.**

55. Thomas Magnell, Editor, *Explorations of Value.*

56. HPP (Hennie) Lötter, Injustice, *Violence, and Peace: The Case of South Africa.* A volume in **Philosophy of Peace.**

57. Lennart Nordenfelt, *Talking About Health: A Philosophical Dialogue.* A volume in **Nordic Value Studies.**

58. Jon Mills and Janusz A. Polanowski, *The Ontology of Prejudice.* A volume in **Philosophy and Psychology.**

59. Leena Vilkka, *The Intrinsic Value of Nature.*

60. Palmer Talbutt, Jr., *Rough Dialectics: Sorokin's Philosophy of Value*, with Contributions by Lawrence T. Nichols and Pitirim A. Sorokin.

61. C. L. Sheng, *A Utilitarian General Theory of Value.*

62. George David Miller, *Negotiating Toward Truth: The Extinction of Teachers and Students.* Epilogue by Mark Roelof Eleveld. A volume in **Philosophy of Education.**

63. William Gerber, *Love, Poetry, and Immortality: Luminous Insights of the World's Great Thinkers.*

64. Dane R. Gordon, Editor, *Philosophy in Post-Communist Europe.* A volume in **Post-Communist European Thought.**

65. Dane R. Gordon and Józef Niżnik, Editors, *Criticism and Defense of Rationality in Contemporary Philosophy*. A volume in **Post-Communist European Thought.**

66. John R. Shook, *Pragmatism: An Annotated Bibliography, 1898-1940.* With Contributions by E. Paul Colella, Lesley Friedman, Frank X. Ryan, and Ignas K. Skrupskelis.

67. Lansana Keita, *The Human Project and the Temptations of Science.*

68. Michael M. Kazanjian, *Phenomenology and Education: Cosmology, Co-Being, and Core Curriculum.* A volume in **Philosophy of Education.**

69. James W. Vice, *The Reopening of the American Mind: On Skepticism and Constitutionalism.*

70. Sarah Bishop Merrill, *Defining Personhood: Toward the Ethics of Quality in Clinical Care.*

71. Dane R. Gordon, *Philosophy and Vision.*

72. Alan Milchman and Alan Rosenberg, Editors, *Postmodernism and the Holocaust.* A volume in **Holocaust and Genocide Studies.**

73. Peter A. Redpath, *Masquerade of the Dream Walkers: Prophetic Theology from the Cartesians to Hegel.* A volume in **Studies in the History of Western Philosophy.**

74. Malcolm D. Evans, *Whitehead and Philosophy of Education: The Seamless Coat of Learning.* A volume in **Philosophy of Education.**

75. Warren E. Steinkraus, *Taking Religious Claims Seriously: A Philosophy of Religion*, edited by Michael H. Mitias. A volume in **Universal Justice.**

76. Thomas Magnell, Editor, *Values and Education.*

77. Kenneth A. Bryson, *Persons and Immortality.* A volume in **Natural Law Studies**.

78. Steven V. Hicks, *International Law and the Possibility of a Just World Order: An Essay on Hegel's Universalism.* A volume in **Universal Justice.**

79. E.F. Kaelin, *Texts on Texts and Textuality: A Phenomenology of Literary Art*, edited by Ellen J. Burns.

80. Amihud Gilead, *Saving Possibilities: A Study in Philosophical Psychology*, A volume in **Philosophy and Psychology**.

81. André Mineau, *The Making of the Holocaust: Ideology and Ethics in the Systems Perspective*. A volume in **Holocaust and Genocide Studies**.

82. Howard P. Kainz, *Politically Incorrect Dialogues: Topics Not Discussed in Polite Circles.*

83. Veikko Launis, Juhani Pietarinen, and Juha Räikkä, Editors, *Genes and Morality: New Essays*. A volume in **Nordic Value Studies**.

84. Steven Schroeder, *The Metaphysics of Cooperation: A Study of F. D. Maurice.*

85. Caroline Joan ("Kay") S. Picart, *Thomas Mann and Friedrich Nietzsche: Eroticism, Death, Music, and Laughter*. A volume in **Central-European Value Studies**.

86. G. John M. Abbarno, Editor, *The Ethics of Homelessness: Philosophical Perspectives.*

87. James Giles, Editor, *French Existentialism: Consciousness, Ethics, and Relations with Others*. A volume in **Nordic Value Studies**.

88. Deane Curtin and Robert Litke, Editors, *Institutional Violence*. A volume in **Philosophy of Peace**.

89. Yuval Lurie, *Cultural Beings: Reading the Philosophers of* Genesis.

90. Sandra A. Wawrytko, Editor, *The Problem of Evil: An Intercultural Exploration*. A volume in **Philosophy and Psychology**.

91. Gary J. Acquaviva, *Values, Violence, and Our Future*. A volume in **Hartman Institute Axiology Studies**.

92. Michael R. Rhodes, *Coercion: A Nonevaluative Approach.*

93. Jacques Kriel, *Matter, Mind, and Medicine: Transforming the Clinical Method.*

94. Haim Gordon, *Dwelling Poetically: Educational Challenges in Heidegger's Thinking on Poetry*. A volume in **Philosophy of Education**.

95. Ludwig Grünberg, *The Mystery of Values: Studies in Axiology*, edited by. Cornelia Grünberg, and Laura Grünberg.